Suppre
Medical
Science

The Key to Lower Cost

&

Higher Quality Health Care

Jack Phillips

Founding Director:

**Freedom of Choice in Medical Care
Foundation**

Suppressed Medical Science
ISBN 10: 1-59152-077-0
ISBN 13: 978-1-59152-077-1

Published by John J. Phillips
© 2011 by John J. Phillips

You may order extra copies of this book by calling Farcountry Press toll free at (800) 821-3874.

Produced by:

Sweetgrass Books
A Division of Farcountry Press
P. O. Box 5630
Helena, MT 59604
(800) 821-3874
Printed in the United States.
15 14 13 12 11 1 2 3 4 5 6 7

PURCHASE FROM:
www.farcountypress.com
(800) 821-3874
www.suppressedmedicalscience.com
or
www.rush2013.com

ABOUT THE AUTHOR.

John J. (Jack) Phillips, SB '38, SM '40, MBA'51, Major USAR; Retired, was born in New York City in 1917. He studied Chemical Engineering at MIT and Business Administration at Harvard. Called to active duty in January 1941, he served almost five years as an Ordnance Officer, returning home after 3 and 1/2 years overseas, on VJ Day.

He has had industrial experience in the petroleum, textile, and electronics industries. A life-long learner, he developed one of the first chromatographic instruments for analysis of petroleum products in his own company.

He was involved with the Jupiter, Redstone, and Pershing Missile industrial programs in Office, Chief of Ordnance in the Pentagon, and with the Nike and Anti-Tank Missile programs at the Army Rocket and Guided Missile Agency in Huntsville, Alabama.

At NASA Headquarters, he was associated with the Mercury, Gemini, and Apollo programs; and the Office of Advanced Research and Technology from which he retired.

He remains an emeritus member of both the American Chemical Society and Sigma Xi.

TABLE OF CONTENTS

ACKNOWLEDGMENTS

I credit the organizational skills of my friend Stephen Miller of Blairsville, Georgia with getting me started on this book. He also suggested that a Constitutional Amendment was needed to solve our medical care problems. It is appropriate that it be called The Rush Amendment [1] because it was Dr. Benjamin Rush who foresaw, in 1787, the need for Constitutional protection of the natural right of Americans to freedom of choice in medical care.

I owe a great deal to Mrs. Alice W. Phillips of St. Petersburg, Florida who edited a draft version of this book and made many helpful suggestions and to Mrs. Marilyn Ann Ellsworth, of Gulfport, FL, who prepared the manuscript for publication.

I am indebted to Mary Genevieve Clarkson whose unstinting devotion to my care and welfare made my research and writing far easier than it would otherwise have been.

Jack Phillips,
St Petersburg, Florida
January 2011

---

[1] Go to www.rush2013.com for information on The Dr. Benjamin Rush Amendment Project.

INTRODUCTION

This book is intended to provide readers with information about the development of the most expensive, poor quality medical care system in the world, which our political leaders are trying to institutionalize with universal medical insurance. It is not an indictment of hard working physicians who are doing their best to provide the best possible care to their patients under difficult circumstances. But it is intended to be an indictment of the undercover dictatorship that has been controlling the practice of medicine for over 100 years and continually increasing their share of the Gross National Product of the United States.

As predicted in 1787, by Dr. Benjamin Rush, this undercover dictatorship, in the absence of Constitutional protection of the right to freedom of choice in medical care continues to restrict choices of medical treatments available to the public, as well as limiting the medical treatments that providers of medical services can offer. They have used this power to prevent physicians from providing more effective treatments developed by medical scientists that promised lower costs and less damage to patients. For example they induced the Federal Food and Drug Administration to declare technology, developed by Royal R. Rife, illegal to use and to confiscate Rife equipment out of physicians' offices.

The Monopoly's power derives from enabling legislation and cooperative government regulation. With Congressional grants of control of medical education, and the practice of medicine, and hundreds of millions of dollars for lobbying and campaign contributions, their power is strongly entrenched. Petitioning Congress for relief is very unlikely to result in any action. On the other hand individual states can act in their own behalf and, if they act in unison, they can cause change. A demand of the People in every state for enactment of an amendment to the Constitutions to ensure freedom of choice in medical care would be hard to ignore.

CHAPTER 1 - OVERVIEW

At about $7,000 per person per year, Americans have the most expensive medical care in the world. Prices continue to rise faster than the cost of living. Health care expenses exceeded $2 trillion in 2009. This is 17% of our Gross National Product. Medical expenses are bankrupting businesses, federal and state governments, and 700,000 US citizens per year [2].

In 2008, a poll taken during the election revealed that only 18% of US citizens were satisfied with our health care system. In response, recent National Health Care legislation "solved" the problem. The new law markedly expands the number of people who can be expected to be paying customers of our health care providers by forcing everybody to buy health care insurance. Cost controls are still nonexistent because no public option was included.

The Congressional Budget Office has advised that the retirement of 80 million Baby Boomers over the next 20 years will cause additional severe fiscal problems for the Social Security and Medicare Programs, which are already on shaky ground. We have only some 40 million people in the Social Security Program now, but budget troubles are an annual affair. With double as many people to cover, fulfilling the needs of so many will require one of two things: either a drastic reduction in the cost of medical care, or a

---

[2] D Himmelstein et. al., *Health Affairs Web Exclusive* 2/2/2005 pp W5-62.

11

significant reduction in the amount of that care. In simple terms, either you get more for your money, or you make do with less because you can't afford it. Medical insurance works the same way. It isn't going to magically make health care affordable. Health insurance premiums are already very high, and rising, because insurance companies don't operate at a loss. When their costs rise, so do your premiums. Government subsidization of health insurance premiums only passes the cost on to taxpayers - a good deal for the insurance companies; not so good a deal for the taxpayers.

We are told regularly that we have the best health care in the world - possibly to persuade us into paying the highest rate for it. Politicians claim that our healthcare is great! If we pay the highest prices in the world, we should expect the product to be of the highest quality: right?

Unfortunately, according to the World Health Organization's [W.H.O.] *World Health Report 2000*, quality of the product delivered was said to be comparatively low. We were number 37 on a list of 191 members of the United Nations where Japan is said to provide the best medical care. A more recent, but smaller, W.H.O. study ranked the US 15th out of the 25 industrialized nations studied. A 2001 Harvard School of Public Health comparison of national health care systems in 17 countries, based on patients' public opinion polls, ranked the US as number 14 and gave France first place. In 2006, the Commonwealth Fund, a private research organization in New York, concluded that the US Health Care System was not the best in the world, nor is it a leader in health information technology.

12

Iatrogenic disease is our third leading cause of death after heart disease and cancer. The term iatrogenic is defined as "induced in a patient by a physician's activity, manner, or therapy: used especially to pertain to a complication of treatment." Over 200,000 deaths every year may be attributable to medical treatment, more than half attributed to care received in a hospital! In addition, over 2 million people may have been maimed and disabled every year. [3,4,5]. Deaths caused by drugs properly prescribed, and taken, may have killed about 100,000 of us every year for the last 30 years. Those improperly prescribed, or improperly taken, may have caused an additional 80,000 deaths according to the New England Journal of Medicine. When physicians go on strike local death rates decrease!

Furthermore, the overall health of our citizens is deteriorating. Over the past fifty years, new American diseases like autism, chronic fatigue syndrome, and fibromyalgia have been diagnosed and/or appeared out of nowhere. New mental diseases are also being identified at a rapid rate. Many of our children are diagnosed as mentally ill and given psychoactive drugs at school. (The FDA has found drugs used to treat ADHD may contribute to the high incidence of psychotic symptoms including hallucinations). Our children are increasingly affected by asthma, allergies, obesity, and possibly sexual abnormalities. Sperm counts and testosterone levels in American men have been declining for 50 years [6]. If these declines continue

---

[3] B. Starfield, MD, MPH, *JAMA*, July 2000.
[4] Jason et. al., (Kazarou et al.) *JAMA* 279, 4/15/98 pp 1200-1205.
[5] D. W. Bates, *JAMA* 279 4/15/98, pp1216-1217.
[6] Bioidentical Hormones, by Lichten.

13

unabated, we could conceivably lose the ability to reproduce.

WHY IS HEALTH CARE SO EXPENSIVE?

First, there is waste, fraud, and abuse in our system. The Life Extension Foundation estimates that payments to dead doctors, and similar frauds, use about 20% of total health care program dollars. They estimate that another 20% goes for politically directed extra costs such as mandated rental of oxygen equipment instead of purchase. In addition, insurance margins amount to another 20%. Evidently Americans could save about a trillion dollars a year by paying their own bills.

Incidentally, as Jane Orient, MD., states in her book Your Doctor is Not In, so-called health insurance is really a prepaid medical plan. When you buy insurance for your car you protect yourself from the cost of catastrophic damage to the car. The insurance doesn't cover the cost of oil changes, grease jobs, and repairs. It costs insurance companies significant amounts of money to pay bills. Paying a small bill can cost your insurance company a lot more than the bill itself. One physician reported that he bought a $5,000 deductible catastrophic health insurance policy, paid his own small medical bills and saved over $4,500 in one year. Insurance companies are not in business to break even.

The cost of drugs is also an important component of health care costs. Drug company profit margins are substantial. The April 2002 issue of *Life Extension Magazine* contains information about costs of raw materials and pricing of a few well known drugs sold to Americans. There are dramatic differences between costs of the active ingredients and consumer prices as shown below.

BRAND	RETAIL	COST	MARKUP
Celebrex 100mg	$130.27	$0.60	21,700%
Lipitor 29mg	$272.37	$5.80	4,700%
Prozac 20mg	$247.47	$0.11	225,000%

The pharmaceutical industry claims that the prices charged for these drugs can be ascribed to the high costs of research, and the double blind tests which the FDA requires before new drugs can be sold. Nevertheless, the gross margins still provided about $4 billion for advertising and $36 billion for dividends to shareholders in 2007.

The spiraling costs of drugs are the result of 100 years of medical-industrial monopoly established, and subsequently reinforced, by federal and state laws. The large profit margins of drug companies have also enabled them to spend hundreds of millions of dollars a year on congressional relations. Some estimate that over $700 million was lavished on congressional lobbyists in 2009. These companies also provide $300 million a year to the Food and Drug Administration to fund its operations. Another $100 million contribution is contemplated to fund surveillance of drug company TV advertising. Evidently, the FDA has a vested interest in the continued profitability of drug companies: it is dependent on their profits for its operating expenses.

Physicians, too, are very well paid. Presently a general practitioner makes about $200,000 per year and a back surgeon about $600,000 per year according to Blue Cross/Blue Shield. Some aver that the American

Medical Association [AMA], from its beginnings, aimed to limit the number of practicing physicians in the United States and thereby increase their incomes by monopolistic means. The AMA's ethics also discouraged competition between members which permitted the institution of simultaneous increases in fees for medical services. It delivered on the promises it had made to encourage membership. Soon, physicians who had previously been members of the lower middle class in 1900, were making 5½ times as much as an average working person by 1925.

Increased educational requirements for entry to medical school and higher medical school tuition made acquisition of a license to practice medicine much more expensive in 1925 than it had been in 1900. Before 1900, some medical schools charged only $150 per semester and made a profit. Recently, cost per student in a new medical school was estimated to be $130,000 per year: much more than expected tuition charges.

Another factor is the cost of medical malpractice. While the financial impact of malpractice lawsuits, claims, and insurance premiums has been calculated to be only about 2% of total health care costs in this country, the impact on individual doctors and other professionals at risk of being sued is substantial. Many physicians have retired early, or simply stopped practicing medicine, in response to the threatening legal environment that has been created. Malpractice insurance premiums have skyrocketed since 2000, sometimes by as much as 20% to 25% a year, according to Boston Globe reports. The way doctors practice medicine has certainly been affected by the threat of lawsuits. Tests are ordered as "defensive medicine" for fear that failure to cover every angle might result in big trouble. Obstetricians, general surgeons, and internists have been particularly hard hit. Hospitals, too, can be the target of malpractice suits, increasing operating costs, and reducing profitability. Because of industry-wide cost cutting, doctors today are spending less time with patients, and hospitals are providing care with fewer and fewer nurses. Most people within the medical industry will agree that standards of care have been compromised, at least to a degree. Arguably, this can lead to even more lawsuits.

Medical devices, everything from plastic tubing to multi-million dollar X-Ray, and CT and MRI scanners, are also comparatively much more expensive than similar non-medical equipment. Device manufacturers' mark up products intended for sale to the health care market, and often cite the need for special testing or approvals as a justification. Legal liability exposure is doubtless also on their minds.

A SHORT HISTORY OF AMERICAN MEDICINE

During the fourth century BC, Hippocrates established his famous medical center on the Greek island of Cos. During his lifetime he welcomed any student who could pay the tuition, but after his death fierce competition developed among his disciples for students and patients. The Hippocratic Oath [7], formulated by Hippocrates' followers after his death, pledged devoted care to the sick, but also contained the first recorded attempt to institutionalize a medical

---

[7] See Appendix 1.

monopoly. Those who took the oath promised to share their knowledge and understanding with only a select few. Each man would pass his secrets on "to my sons, to those of my teachers, and to those pupils duly apprenticed and sworn, and to none others."

From the time of Hippocrates, two schools of medicine grew side by side [8] One in which patients were treated as unique individuals, the other in which the disease, rather than the patient, determined the treatment. Establishment medicine in America has favored the second school from its beginnings.

In the early days of the American Republic, there were about 100 European-trained allopathic physicians treating Americans. They served in the armed services and the larger communities which could afford them. Their therapies were not popular. They believed that unhealthy blood was the cause of many diseases. Bleeding, even of infants in arms, to remove causes of disease from the body, was their common practice. In addition, 'medicinal' remedies considered to have significant therapeutic value, such as mercury chloride, arsenic, opium and quinine, were popularly used on patients by physicians. Dr. Benjamin Rush, a prominent Philadelphia physician, signer of the Declaration of Independence, and a Surgeon General in George Washington's Continental Army, was a leading proponent of these therapies. But after the Revolutionary War, he proposed that freedom of choice in medical care be installed in the Constitution. He was concerned that physicians less principled than himself might seek to establish a sort of medical dictatorship

---

[8] Divided Legacy, by Harris L. Coulter.

18

along the lines of England's Royal College of Physicians [RPC], a long established and state-approved medical monopoly. Dr. Rush knew his history. In 1765, John Morgan had tried to start an inter-colonial medical licensing agency in Philadelphia, based on the RCP. Colonial doctors would not agree, and the proposal failed. Morgan did establish the first American medical school, however, where, in keeping with European medical traditions, the "regular mode of practice" was firmly set as the dominant orthodoxy. Innovation was strictly frowned upon.

After the Revolution, medical licensing amounted to little more than a prestigious honorific for conventionally trained physicians. In the frontier environment of the early days there were few physicians or regulatory agencies, and alternative therapies such as herbal medicine based on American Indian lore flourished. Samuel Thompson, a self taught New Hampshire farmer developed a simplified medical system involving steam baths, an emetic, and herbs. He patented it, and sold rights to use it for $20. An estimated 1 million Americans were using his system in the mid 1800s. Unschooled herbalists like Jacob Tidd of New Jersey also served the public. They joined the Thomasonians to form eclectic schools of medicine using the best of available medical doctrines. In 1820, the Reformed Medical School was established in New York, bringing the number of eclectic medical schools in the United States up to 12.

Few people realize that American medicine underwent its own revolution in the 1850's. Competition, principally from eclectic and homeopathic physicians, provided kinder and gentler therapies that were far less damaging and lethal than those practiced by traditional physicians who used the lancet as their primary tool. During the 1830's, establishment physicians in both France and the United States were challenged by cholera epidemics which decimated the afflicted. At that time, some said that if the disease didn't kill you the doctor would, but in both countries, physicians trained in the new, patient-centered art of Homeopathy performed extremely well. Homeopathic physicians outperformed the monopoly allopaths during the cholera epidemics and subsequently in a yellow fever epidemic in the Mississippi valley. As a result, establishment physicians became unpopular, and Americans: farmers, tradesmen and laborers, organized and demanded the repeal of medical licensing laws. In the free-market environment of the 1850's, one state after another repealed penalties against unlicensed practice.

Homeopathy became very popular because its medications were relatively benign and its practitioners, medical doctors given further training in the art of homeopathy, had proven their effectiveness. This advancement in the science of medicine was discovered by Samuel Hahneman, a German Physician. He quit practicing medicine to study the effects of medication on healthy people. His research revealed that medicines that cured diseases *caused* the symptoms of these diseases in healthy people and that small quantities worked better than large quantities. The crowned heads and aristocracy in Europe and the United States accepted this new modality. John D. Rockefeller was a homoeopathist, as is the present Queen of England. Boston was a hotbed of homeopathy.

In 1845, the Cincinnati Eclectic Medical Institute opened. Homeopathic physicians established an

American association in 1846. The regular physicians formed the American Medical Association in 1847 with 255 members. By the middle of the 19th century, although the majority of physicians were still the traditional, European-style Allopaths, virtually no government barriers existed in the practice of medicine. Lassaiz-faire policies extended everywhere and, as might be expected, opportunities abounded. Along with the Allopaths, Homeopaths, and Eclectics were a motley variety of quacks and snake-oil salesmen. Medical treatment was cheap and easy to obtain. Unfortunately, it was sometimes ineffective, and at worst it could be deadly.

Many physicians were poor. Orthodox physicians who taught in medical schools began making more money than regular practitioners. With the cost of education low - about $150 per semester - poor whites, and blacks in the South, could become doctors. Soon there was about one physician for every 530 people in the United States, twice as many per capita as there were in Germany. The resulting competition lowered medical costs. Eclectic (herbal) medicine, homeopathy and other varieties of medical treatments were readily available. An eclectic physician, Eli Jones, cured his first cancer case in 1869. He became the expert whom other physicians sought when they developed the disease. He cured over 80% of previously untreated cancer patients. In his opinion cancer was a systemic disease, and cancer surgery, therefore, was malpractice.

From time to time various groups of doctors attempted to standardize fees among themselves, but such efforts were generally failures. There was simply too much competition to support price-fixing. Some of

21

this competition came from nefarious characters with neither morals nor medical knowledge and this formed the basis for a backlash against "quackery." Subsequently, the American Medical Association used this backlash for its own purposes.

In spite of the wide availability of physician's services, or perhaps partly because of them, the general quality of American health was relatively poor. American soldiers of that time were reported to be smaller than European soldiers, and loss of teeth was not uncommon. European visitors made derogatory remarks about the physical appearance of Americans. In 1856, *Harper's Monthly* noted that Americans were "a pale, pasty faced, narrow-chested, spindle-shanked, dwarfed race." The War Department disclosed that Americans recruited for the Mexican War weighed less than Europeans and they were much more frequently rejected due to their poor physical condition, or malformed and contracted chests. Women and girls were mostly invalids according to Thomas Wentworth Higginson in 1861. Many people were toothless from doses of calomel [9] they received throughout their lives. Bloodletting was still widely used, even for childhood diseases, until the end of the century, and many children died as a result. Not surprisingly, the competing medical systems continued to flower until the beginning of the 20th century.

Throughout most of the last half of the 19th

---

9 Calomel, also called mercurous chloride, or mercury (i) chloride (Hg_2Cl_2), a very heavy, soft, white, sweetish-tasting halide mineral, formed by the alteration of other mercury minerals, such as cinnabar or amalgams. Calomel is usually found naturally together with native mercury, cinnabar, calcite, limonite, and clay.

Century, competition kept prices for medical services low. The glut of physicians, popular competing modalities, and the very real hazard of quackery provided a rational basis for action, and organized medicine began lobbying against new doctors and new therapies. The American Medical Association started small but operated to improve member incomes and eliminate competition. It would use whatever methods were available, and with the example provided by the Royal College of Physicians as a guide, the AMA went to work.

The strategy, designed by Nathan Smith Davis, was to establish state licensing boards which would be operated by medical societies. Davis condemned medical schools for irresponsibly expanding the number of physicians for the primary purpose of enriching themselves. He proposed to restrict entry to, and competition between, medical schools by forming regulatory boards - staffed, of course, by members of the AMA. By 1900, every state again had strict medical licensing laws.

In 1883, the *Journal of the American Medical Association* [*JAMA*] replaced its former publication, called Transactions, and trustees decided that advertisements for patent medicines would be excluded. Patent medicine companies, many of which were founded during the Civil War, had done the old snake oil salesmen one better by selling professionally packaged products, with secret and proprietary formulas, which were advertised as cures for a wide variety of ills and complaints, from stomach ache to baldness. They made money, too. This created a dilemma for *JAMA's* editors. Facing competition from about 250 professional journals directly supported by drug companies, they must have eventually compromised because in 1892 the Philadelphia County Medical Society reported a strong vote of censure against *JAMA* for advertising secret remedies. In 1894, the trustees noted that complying with the wishes of the Philadelphia society would result in a loss for which the trustees would be responsible. In 1895, the Penn State Medical Society brought an action against the trustees for continuing unethical advertising. The AMA's judicial council decided that there had been some questionable advertising and that the trustee's new rule required the name and quantity of each ingredient of the advertised product to be included in the advertisement. Advertising income is reported to have dropped to between $12,000 and $13,000 dollars a year and it cost $25,000 (Estimated $750,000 in 2010 dollars) to produce the Journal.

In 1899, when Dr. George Simmons of Lincoln, Nebraska was appointed editor of their Journal, AMA headquarters and the Journal's staff were housed in a single rented room. Advertising revenues were $33,700 with 13,000 subscribers and reorganization was planned. Simmons was appointed secretary of the reorganization committee.

In 1900, there were about 15,000 homeopathic and a lesser number of eclectic physicians in the United States, most of whom prospered, and some 100,000 regular allopathic physicians, many of whom still struggled financially. But the hard times would not last for long, as new medical discoveries in Europe provided the basis for big changes in America.

Late in the 19th century, Louis Pasteur in France, and Friedrich Koch in Germany, laid the foundations for Scientific Medicine based on the Germ Theory of

Disease. This theory assumes that the body is sterile and it is microorganisms that enter it which cause diseases. It was controversial at its beginnings. Claude Bernard, an eminent physiologist, maintained that germs were everywhere and the internal condition of the body determined whether or not they caused disease. Furthermore, Antoine Bechamp, an eminent professor of medicine at the University of Lille, discovered that tiny microorganisms, that he called microzymas, present in every cell, could metamorphose into disease-causing organisms inside the body. Despite his discovery, and in the face of much opposition, the Germ Theory was accepted by the allopathic medical community and Scientific Medicine and laboratories for medical research proliferated.

Ilya I. Metchnikoff, winner of a Nobel Prize in medicine, and one of the proponents of the Germ Theory, agreed that it would be invalid if people could be found who harbored disease-causing microorganisms without exhibiting symptoms of the disease. Both Koch and Pasteur are reported to have found such people. Typhoid Mary [10] also met the criteria. Nevertheless, American Medical Association executives welcomed the advent of Scientific Medicine and saw in it an opportunity to better the economic

---

10 Mary Mallon (September 23, 1869 – November 11, 1938), also known as "Typhoid Mary," was the first person in the United States to be identified as a healthy carrier of typhoid fever. Over the course of her career as a cook, she is known to have infected 53 people, three of whom died from the disease. Her notoriety is in part due to her vehement denial of her own role in spreading the disease, together with her refusal to cease working as a cook. She was forcibly quarantined twice by public health authorities and died in quarantine.

condition of their members, and once again control their environment. It was powerless to do so until it was reorganized and allied itself with the drug industry. For its first 50 years, the AMA had been a democratic self-governed body of professional men. Its efforts were enough to convince the various States to reintroduce licensing requirements for physicians, but it lacked the funding and political clout to further advance its agenda. The advent of scientific medicine, stemming from the work of the Europeans Koch and Pasteur, provided it with an opportunity to further improve the reputation and economic status of its members.

In 1901, the AMA reorganized into a three tiered structure, where ordinary members had little power. In effect, it became The Physicians Union. Management had a free hand. In 1902, Simmons moved into a new, concrete and steel, seven-story building in a prestigious Chicago location and ultimately staffed it with 300 people. With the purse strings safely in his hands, Doc Simmons, who earned an MD in 1882 at the Hahnemann Medical College, a homeopathic institution, proceeded to enlarge the AMA's power and influence. Delicate negotiations with the drug companies were reported and soon *JAMA* turned into a gold mine. Advertising income rose to $88,500 in 1903 and reached $150,000 in 1909. This was enough to pay all the Association's expenses and generate a large surplus. Subscriptions rose to 80,000 in 1910.

With only 9,000 out of 100,000 potential members enrolled in 1899, the Association had little influence. More members were needed. AMA's recruiters promised physicians: "Join our Union and we will raise your pay." Since the average physician was

26

earning about $750 per year, this offer was persuasive. By 1904, recruitment efforts tripled membership to 30,000 and, by 1925, a majority of "regular" physicians in private practice in the United States were enrolled. Soon, almost every physician in the country was a member.

From the outset the Association had focused on reducing competition. Cutting the number of medical schools, increasing requirements for entry to them and increasing tuition were objectives. Moving towards control of medical education, the AMA proposed that all medical students should have a suitable preliminary education, and that a uniform set of requirements should be adopted in all medical schools. In 1904, it established a Permanent Council on Medical Education. In 1905, the Council arranged a conference of State medical licensing boards to review the status of medical education and set standards for medical schools. In 1906, its Council on Medical Education reviewed the quality of medical education in 160 medical schools, giving 82 of them an 'A,' 46 a 'B,' and 32 a 'C'.

In 1907, Arthur D. Bevan, the Council's chairman, convinced Henry Prichard, former President of MIT, who headed the Carnegie Foundation, to sponsor a comprehensive study of medical education. In November of that year, Prichard's trustees approved the study and Abraham Flexner, a graduate of Johns Hopkins University with no medical experience but a background in education, was hired to conduct it. Abraham Flexner was, however, the brother of Simon Flexner, a director of the Rockefeller Institute for Medical Research. Abraham Flexner was accompanied during the study by the new chairman of the AMA's Council, Nathan Caldwell. They visited all the medical

27

schools in the United States. They started with Johns Hopkins, which had recently installed laboratories for medical research like those in Germany. Many other medical schools did not meet Flexner's standards, including the recently modernized Harvard Medical School. Flexner's final report, co-authored by Caldwell, was issued in 1910. Some suggest that it was a rewrite of the Council's 1906 review of medical schools. It recommended closure of a large number of medical schools, raising standards of the remainder, and reducing enrollments of students. A college degree instead of a high school diploma was required for entry, and schools had to have research laboratories. Acting on the recommendations of The Flexner Report, legislatures began to close non-AMA-approved medical schools, further restricting entry into the profession.

The teaching of Scientific Medicine was intended to be capital intensive. Equipping and supplying medical laboratories, and other new requirements, increased costs significantly. Tuition and fees were no longer sufficient to support the operation of schools and could not be raised beyond the capability of students to pay them. Those schools that were unable to obtain grants and bequests were forced to consolidate or close. The prosperous homeopathic competitors of the AMA took a big hit. In 1906, there were 163 medical schools. In 1910, the number was reduced from 166 to 131; in 1920, 85. Only 63 remained in 1929. Flexner was convinced that Hahnemann was a fraud. John D. Rockefeller's distributor of gifts, Frederick Gates, wrote that Hahnemann was insane. Homeopathic schools found it all but impossible to raise capital for investments required by the new standards. Even though John D. Rockefeller was a homoeopathist and wanted some of his money to support homeopathy, none of it did. John D., Jr. told his father that the homeopaths were integrating with the allopaths. One homeopathic school's letters of request to Rockefeller for funds were said to have been unanswered. By this means the AMA disposed of its most effective competition, and Americans were deprived of a technology which had proved its superiority during cholera and yellow fever epidemics. After 1930, even the Hahnemann Medical College of Philadelphia was teaching allopathic medicine except for one or two classes of homeopathy. In the 1930s and 1940s, eleven homeopathic schools closed. During the great depression, the AMA ordered medical schools to admit fewer students. Every school followed instructions rather than risk losing their AMA accreditation. The number of physicians practicing medicine in the US dropped gradually as death and retirement winnowed the ranks and fewer new physicians graduated from the remaining medical schools.

The fledgling monopolists of the 1850's had finally found the means to put themselves in power. With the restoration of medical licensing laws, effective control of medical education, and with funds flowing in, they convinced upper and middle class people that they could bring the wondrous benefits of science to their patients. At least $300,000,000 ($600,000,000 according to Coulter's Divided Legacy) was contributed by wealthy donors to fund the medical revolution. Philanthropist John D. Rockefeller took a special interest because one of his grandsons had died of scarlet fever in 1901 and a prominent physician had told him that there was no cure for the disease. In 1901, John D.

founded the Rockefeller Institute for Medical Research and funded it with $1,000,000 that same year. The drug industry also funneled advertising money through *JAMA* to help them regain control. At a time when one dollar bought a 10 hour day's work, this was an irresistible flood; it carried orthodox physicians back into power.

State legislatures gave the Association responsibility for establishing standards for medical education. Now, in order to become a practicing physician, students had to graduate from AMA approved schools. In effect, the Association won the power to dictate what medical students were taught. Curricula were heavy on science, but there was only minimal training in pharmacology and nutrition. Physicians who used to make their own remedies began to rely on pharmaceutical companies for the drugs they prescribed and for information about them. AMA membership rose by almost 900%.

AMA's ethical standards forbade competition between members and the executives arranged for periodic, unannounced increases in fees to be charged by members. The strategy worked well. The annual income of physicians has risen much faster than inflation over the past 100 years, and physicians, as a class, are now quite wealthy in comparison to other unionized groups.

With the rise of the American Medical Association during the first half of the 20th century, the practice of medicine took on the character of a business. With its allies in the Food and Drug Administration and pharmaceutical industry, the AMA progressively cemented its control over the nature and conduct of the medical establishment, increasing profits and decreasing competition wherever, and whenever, possible. Standards were established and maintained, and all components of the monopoly enjoyed large profits. The AMA's income also benefitted, as advertising revenue from *JAMA* far surpassed annual dues as an income source. Even today, although less than 20% of practicing physicians are members now, it generates two-thirds of its $230 million operating budget from non-dues sources.

A major source of income is its copyrighted Current Procedural Terminology (CPT) code which describes medical services provided to patients. In 1983, an agreement between the Health Care Financing Administration and the AMA established the CPT Code as the only coding system for billing Medicare. This takes care of allopathic physicians operating under the Standards of Care, but leaves over 4 million alternative and integrative medical practitioners out in the cold with no means for billing Medicare. In 1997, the US court of Appeals for the Ninth District decided that the exclusive agreement with the HCFA provided the AMA with an unfair advantage and involved a misuse of its copyright.

When queried by Senator Trent Lot about coding problems in 2001, the Department of Health and Human Services approved a two-year pilot project which permitted the use of the ABC codes. This independent coding system covers 4400 new items consistent with the needs of alternative and integrative health care providers and complements the CPT codes. It was successful but, although the AMA appears willing to cooperate, the Federal government is balking at changes that affect the health care billing system.

Since physicians can be charged with a crime for

billing an "unnecessary treatment" to Medicare or a private insurance company, this coding problem is important. Some physicians choose not to participate in any government plan, or accept private insurance payments, to avoid trouble. Another option is to use ABC codes which can automatically convert to the AMA code's close equivalents.

Between 1988 and 1998, US health-care costs increased 74.4 percent. Congress was co-operative and sympathetic - and well compensated for their troubles. Health care became Big Business. Now, consistent with the political concept of medicine as a business, a six-digit number assigned by the diagnosing physician determines the treatment and, if the McKesson Company [11] gets its way, an approved "drug." This "one size fits all" brand of medicine is inconsistent with the concept of healing as a sacred art. It prevents healers from practicing their arts as their judgment dictates and it prevents patients from choosing competing modalities that they may want and need. There is more than one way to treat a disease, just as there is more than one way to catch it.

HOW AMA OBTAINED CONTROL OF HOSPITALS

Remember when doctors made house calls? Medical services were, at one time, available whenever you needed them, and the doctor would come to you with his little black bag. If you were sick, or injured, and needed medical attention, you didn't have to worry

---

[11] McKesson is a very large company in the drug business.

about getting to the hospital. About 1918, a surgeon, and the obstetrician who delivered me, laid me on the kitchen table in my family's apartment, put a food strainer over my face, covered it with a dishcloth, poured ether on the cloth to put me to sleep, and proceeded to circumcise me.

There were few hospitals in the country prior to 1900, but once the AMA began to establish its monopoly, many were built to provide workspace for physicians. Control of hospitals became a new objective. Legislatures were induced to add internship and residency requirements to licensing laws and give the AMA responsibility for approving hospitals for this training. Hospitals wanted this approval because it provided cheap labor for them. They offered no resistance to requirements that they limit their staffs to members of local medical societies. This forced most practicing physicians to join the local societies and adopt their code of ethics which proscribed activities which might threaten the welfare of other members, like price cutting, advertising, and the like. Violators could be punished by expulsion from the local society with loss of staff status in hospitals. This would be the kiss of death for their careers, although they could still practice independently as long as they did not create serious public problems.

When one Congressman opposed the Association's legislative objectives, members were assessed $25 each to fund a successful drive to prevent his reelection. This convinced others to "go along to get along" and political influence was established.

In effect the State legislatures abdicated their authority in favor of the AMA. Economist Ruben A. Kessel opined that: "Delegation by state legislatures to the AMA of the power to regulate the medical industry in the public interest is on a par with giving the American Iron and Steel Institute the power to determine the output of steel."

Limiting the number of practicing physicians is keeping many of them busier than they want to be. And other factors have become involved. Medical malpractice lawsuits have become increasingly prevalent, and profitable, over the years, prompting many doctors to retire early or to simply close shop. The resultant reduction in the availability of care has further driven up the price of that care.

INSTALLATION OF SCIENTIFIC MEDICINE

The search for magic bullets to kill invading microbes resulted in the discovery of sulpha drugs and penicillin. By the end of World War II they gave allopathic physicians an overwhelming advantage over their competitors. These medications were quickly effective against infectious diseases, but even then some bacteria were developing resistance to them. Subsequent overuse has created difficult new problems. Antibiotic-resistant bacteria are now infecting patients in our hospitals. Some patients are in worse condition when they leave than they were when they entered the hospital.

On close examination, what has been called scientific medicine is not so scientific after all. Only about 15% of medical procedures currently in use have been proven by the gold standard double blind testing that the FDA requires before it gives approval of new medications and procedures. This disturbing statistic was discovered by a Congressional Office of Technology Assessment investigation and confirmed by the National Academy of Sciences several years ago.

SUPPRESSED MEDICAL INNOVATIONS

When the drive to increase membership was well underway, Doc Simmons began a crusade against competition which still endures. By his definition, anything other than the practice of orthodox medicine was quackery and those involved were charlatans. The official objective was to protect the public, but quite clearly eliminating competition and controlling the practice of medicine was high on the agenda. Between 1900 and 1925, during Simmons reign, the AMA, with FDA's help, suppressed at least 2 medical innovators: Dinshah Ghardiali, PhD, and William F. Koch, PhD, MD.

Ghardiali, a many talented Persian whiz-kid from India, reportedly made a fortune with a patent on the use of sprockets for movie film. He is said to have spent 30 years developing theory and equipment, the Spectro-chrome and Itsetometer [12], for light therapy. In 1920, he completed development of his therapeutic devices and began teaching physicians and lay people how to use them. In the next 4 years he trained 800 people. In 1924, the AMA took notice with a derogatory article in *JAMA*. This ridiculed Ghadiali and his Spectro-Chrome and closed with: "When it is

---

12 American Free Press, June 11 & 18, 2007: **Whole Body Health**, "The Rise of Modern Medicine; The Downfall of Our Health" by Jack Phillips.

35

realized that helpless but credulous patients are being treated for such serious conditions as syphilitic conjunctivitis, ovaritis, diabetes mellitus, pulmonary tuberculosis, and chronic gonorrhea with colored lights, the space devoted to this latest cult will not be deemed excessive." Subsequently, many physicians stopped using his device.

On October 12, 1926, Dr. Kate Baldwin, who had been senior surgeon at the Philadelphia Women's Hospital for many years, reported, at a Pennsylvania Medical Society meeting, that colored light was the simplest and most accurate therapeutic measure ever developed. She said that she had experimented with this therapy for 6 years and that, after 27 years of medical practice, believed she could produce faster and more accurate results with colored light than with any other method, and with less strain on the patient. She owned several Spectro-Chrome devices and thought that their use in the treatment of burns should be investigated by every member of the profession.

An attempt to have Dinshaw returned to India as a colored alien failed when he was able to prove his Persian ancestry. However, his practice of travelling with his female secretary, even though in a railroad train compartment with the door open at all times, provided his enemies with an opportunity. He was charged with illegally transporting a female across state lines, convicted and jailed. Subsequently, in 1931, Dinshaw was indicted in Buffalo, NY for falsely representing Spectro-Chrome as a healing device. Three physicians and three lay graduates of his course testified in his behalf. The physicians, Drs. Hanor, Baldwin and Peebles, swore that they had successfully treated glaucoma, otitis media, advanced tuberculosis, heart problems, arthritis, tumors, and a host of other conditions with his instrument. The jury decided that Dinshaw, who had defended himself without legal assistance, was not guilty. Ultimately subsequent court actions bankrupted him and the FDA had his books and papers, except for his personal library, burned in a New York City incinerator, and his medical devices were declared illegal to use.

The travails of William F. Koch, PhD, MD, can be found in the Chapter on Cancer in this book and also in Politics in Healing by Daniel Haley, a former member of the New York State Legislature.

MORRIS FISHBEIN'S REIGN

In 1922, Simmons survived a revolt by the Illinois Medical Society, but a personal scandal caused his resignation two years later. By 1925, his protégé, Dr. Morris Fishbein, who couldn't pass his anatomy course and never practiced medicine, was firmly in place as his handpicked successor. Fishbein quickly became a driving force for AMA public relations. A well-oiled publicity machine began issuing an unending stream of propaganda to every available media. His activities as newspaper columnist, medical editor of *Good Housekeeping Magazine*, and advisor for many popular magazines provided contact with science writers. Exploiting an opportunity, the AMA's Board of Trustees hosted a meeting with the National Association of Science Writers in 1937. After the meeting, the following statement was added to the Science Writers code of ethics:

"Science writers are incapable of judging the facts of phenomena involving medical and scientific discovery. Therefore, they only report discoveries approved by medical authorities, or presented before a body of scientific peers."

In 1940, the United Press, headquartered in New York, also accepted AMA censorship of the medical news as evidenced by this bulletin:

"Under no circumstances put any story on the leased wire about a remedy. If the bureau manager is convinced that the story has merit, he should overhead it to New York for investigation and consideration there."

These policies were effective. According to testimony by Arthur Connell, National Commander of the American Legion before the House Committee on Veterans Affairs:

"A contract exists between the State Medical Associations and the newspapers which makes it virtually impossible for the veteran's side of medical questions to reach the reading public."

In his testimony, Connell cited a Denver Post editorial attacking medical aid to war veterans which, on investigation, proved to have been written by an official of the Colorado State Medical Society.

Censorship of the news was of inestimable value to the AMA. Its harassment and persecutions of medical heretics, i.e., anyone engaged in the unorthodox practice of medicine, went unnoticed. The public was prevented from hearing "the other side of the story." Unquestioning acceptance of AMA propaganda allowed the editor of *JAMA* to figuratively get away with murder. However, Harry Hoxsey,

38

founder of the Hoxsey Clinic, ultimately sued him for libel and won.

Fishbein continued Simmon's policy of suppressing medical innovations that the AMA was unable to acquire or control, either for itself or for its drug company allies. Wilhelm Reich, MD, an unusually talented medical scientist whose books were burned by Hitler in Germany, was one of his first victims. In 1937, Reich discovered tiny microbes which caused cancer in mice. He called them T-bacilli. He also discovered a new kind of energy which he named Orgone. This energy had many unusual properties, among them the ability to treat diseases, including cancer, and to change the rate of decay of radium. Medical authorities refused to accept his findings and the FDA charged him with fraud, claiming that there was no such thing as Orgone energy. His books and papers were burned in an incinerator in New York. He died in jail, after being convicted of contempt of court because he maintained that courts of law were not competent to judge scientific issues like whether or not Orgone energy existed.

Fishbein suppressed many other advances in medical science and technology, among them the works of Frederick Klenner, MD, discussed in the Chapter on Contagious Diseases, Harry Hoxsey, Royal Raymond Rife, Virginia Livingston, MD, and Stanislaw Burzinski discussed in the Chapter on Cancer.

Harassment of unconventional medical practitioners continues. It is reported that one third of the physicians practicing alternative medicine in the State of Washington are being harassed. Such interference represents a restraint of trade - forbidden by anti-trust laws.

ALTERNATIVE MEDICAL MODALITIES

A variety of medical modalities are in use in America at this time, but the AMA still has a major role in the operation of the American health care system. The following paragraphs discuss the principal alternatives:

HOMEOPATHY

Almost eliminated from the scene by Scientific Medicine, this modality is once again growing in influence. Samuel Hahnemann MD, a German physician discouraged with orthodox medical practices of his time, developed homeopathy. He discovered that the symptoms produced by quinine in healthy people were similar to those encountered in malaria, and that the symptoms produced by mercury were similar to those encountered in syphilis. Surprisingly, small amounts of quinine were found by experiment to be more effective in curing malaria than the excessively large doses then in common use. Extensive experimentation on himself, his family and friends enabled Hahnemann to publish data on symptoms produced by 27 medications, in 1805. By the end of his life he had gathered such information on 99 medications. Further research disclosed that tiny doses of all of these medications were more effective than large doses for curing diseases of people with symptoms similar to those produced by the same medications in healthy people. In 1825, homeopathic physicians trained in Europe began coming to the United States. They soon became major competitors of the allopathic physicians who were soon forced to offer homeopathic medications to their patients who demanded them.

Negligibly, small doses of medications appeared to enhance the inherent healing power of both animals and humans in some unknown manner. The fact that animals were cured with homeopathic medications proved that they weren't placebos. Research indicates that water has an internal structure which allows it to store information. Nevertheless, it is hard for scientists to believe that extremely dilute homeopathic remedies can be effective. After it came to America in 1825, upper class patients, the best customers for medical services, found small dose homeopathy more acceptable than the bloodletting and massive doses used in allopathy. In Massachusetts, most of the social, intellectual and business elites preferred it. This effective competition earned the enmity of regular physicians.

ISOPATHY

Over 100 years ago, and prior to Pasteur's discovery of bacteria, Antoine Bechamp, a biochemist and Dean of the Faculty at the University of Lille in France, discovered tiny microorganisms, which he called microzymas. They were present in all tissues and in blood, were practically indestructible, and able to change from one form into another. He also found that, when the organism they inhabited died, microzymas turned into fungi and disposed of the tissues.

Guenther Enderline in Germany continued Bechamp's research but renamed microzymas protits. His book Bakterien Cyclogeny earned international acclaim and led to what is called Isopathic Therapy. Some of Enderline's medications have FDA approval and might be useful weapons against the new and lethal antibiotic-resistant bacteria.

One of Enderline's protégés, Franz Friedrich Friedman, MD, developed an isopathic therapy for tuberculosis, which cured over 15,000 patients in Germany before World War I. A Prussian National Assembly Commission investigated Friedmann's therapy and found that it was surprisingly effective on all kinds of tuberculosis, particularly in early stages of the disease. Friedman is reported to have lectured before the US Congress about his discovery, after which President Teddy Roosevelt sent him a letter of appreciation wishing him success in his work. Subsequently, the US Government Printing Office is said to have published a 54-page document titled *"Dr. Friedman's New Treatment for Tuberculosis,"* but Americans were deprived of the potential benefits - faster and less expensive cures. According to newspaper reports, Edward L. Trudeau, MD, who was deeply involved in tuberculosis research and the cottage cure industry in Saranac Lake, NY, led the effort to suppress and discredit Freidman and his "turtle vaccine."

OSTEOPATHY

In 1874, Andrew Taylor Still initiated the practice of osteopathy. Practitioners of this art hold that the musculoskeletal system of the body integrates the action of the body's natural healing power through circulation of the blood. The allopaths vigorously opposed licensing of osteopaths but, since it flourished anyway, the AMA in 1961 began inviting osteopaths to join. By 1990, there were 15 osteopathic schools and

42

about 33,500 practitioners in the United States.

Wilhelm Reich, MD, formerly associated with Sigmund Freud, held that mental and emotional conflicts can be "deposited" in the body's muscular structure as armoring or layering. His theory might explain the observations of osteopaths that patients appear to retrace the feelings and emotions incident to injuries during treatment.

Presently, osteopaths receive training in muscular-skeletal manipulation in addition to the usual training of allopathic physicians. After successful legal action against the persecutions of the AMA, the osteopaths were licensed like ordinary physicians.

CHIROPRACTIC

In 1896, Daniel David Palmer, who had been practicing as a magnetic healer, developed chiropractic based on manipulation of the spinal vertebrae. He maintained that misalignment of the bones in the spine affected the propagation of nervous and mental energy flows, and thus influenced the overall state of the nervous system.

In 1963, the AMA appointed a Committee on Quackery to coordinate the persecution of chiropractors which they called an unscientific cult. They used political influence to restrict access to research funds, educational grants, access to hospitals and insurance coverage. In 1976, the chiropractors fought back with the help of "sore throat", a disgruntled AMA employee who provided them with AMA internal documents. Several practitioners and their organizations sued the AMA and its Quackery Committee with violations of anti-trust laws and won. Judge Susan Getzendanner found that chiropractors outperformed medical physicians in treatment of certain conditions.

In 1992, there were 14 chiropractic schools recognized by the US Office of Education and more than 50,000 practitioners. A Florida study of back and neck injuries in 1960 found that allopathic treatments cost 27% more than chiropractic treatments and their patients lost nine work days instead of three for patients of chiropractors. A New Zealand Commission of Inquiry, in 1979, concluded that chiropractic was not an unscientific cult.

SOMETHING NEEDS TO CHANGE

A reinvigorated medical establishment, utilizing the advanced technologies that the AMA and the FDA have squelched, could substantially reduce medical costs which have spiraled out of control for too long. And costs are not our only concern. Iatrogenic disease, disease caused by medical services, has become the third leading cause of death. Homeopathy and eclectic medicine, eliminated by the AMA, caused few deaths – a good reason to bring them back into service.

The FDA, which receives large sums of money from pharmaceutical companies, has been an effective enforcer for the AMA and their drug company allies. If we allow it to gain more power, there will be little chance to stop the continuing deterioration of our health. Our food supply and our medicines are under their control. For our own safety and the safety of our children, the power of our out-of-control FDA must be reduced.

Isn't it time for an outraged public to clip the wings of both the AMA and the FDA in self defense? It isn't safe to let them retain the power of life and death over us and our children! A "Health Freedom" Constitutional Amendment to ensure freedom of choice in medical care could save both money and lives.

CAN CONGRESS SOLVE OUR HEALTH CARE PROBLEMS?

The historical record shows clearly that we cannot look to Congress for correction of major flaws in our medical care system. The Fitzgerald Report, [13] which has been buried in the Congressional Record for over 50 years, tells a tale of corruption that should long ago have been aired and corrected. The report was requested by Senator Charles Tobey of New Hampshire early in 1953 after he became chairman of the Interstate Commerce Committee (ICC). His son had been cured of lung cancer by unconventional methods. His many attempts to initiate a Congressional investigation of cancer research having been blocked by the AMA. He believed a special investigator could find enough evidence of a conspiracy to force Congress to act despite AMA opposition. Senator Tobey commissioned Benedict F. Fitzgerald, Jr., Special Counsel, US Senate Committee on Interstate and Foreign Commerce to investigate his suspicions.

Unfortunately, Tobey died in July 1953 before the report was finished. The new chairman of the ICC, Senator Bricker of Ohio, was a supporter of the AMA and not only filed the report in a waste basket but

---

13 See Appendix 2.

45

terminated the investigation and had his staff tell Fitzgerald to forget it. Fitzgerald brought the report to the attention of other members of the committee and had it read into the Congressional Record, but lost his job with the Justice Department as a result.

Rather than accepting the deficiencies of our present system of medical care we can seek affordable alternatives with potential for better quality and lower death rates. The historical record indicates that these alternatives exist. Unfortunately, laws that established a medical monopoly 100 years ago, and have increased its power and influence since then, stand in the way. Those laws will be defended tenaciously by the entrenched medical establishment, but our ancestors were able to repeal laws which protected another medical monopoly 150 years ago by joining together in a unified effort.

Medical licensure, as it presently exists, needs to go, and the stranglehold on information and education presently exercised by monopoly interests must be broken. But we as Americans must take responsibility too. We must follow the lead of our ancestors by becoming personally involved in our medical care choices. It is unsafe to leave decisions in the hands of our politicians, who are too easily influenced by money and power, and not prepared by education and experience, to make medical care decisions for us. **Those who have education and experience should be advising us,** *not* **determining things for us.** Unquestioned trust in our doctors and hospitals has led to death or significant deterioration of health for millions of Americans and the toll continues to mount.

Our country cannot afford this disaster. It requires early remediation. Every person is intimately

46

affected by our medical care system and should be involved in changing it to better serve the needs of all the people.

IS THERE A SOLUTION?

Universal Health Insurance is not an effective solution. It can definitely pay bills, and may help control costs, but it does not provide for increased quality of care at lower prices. The results of 100 years of service by our medical monopoly are very unsatisfactory. Our Federal government intends to institutionalize this failing system with mandated universal medical care, but if it is successfully institutionalized, what is the probable result?

The power of this monopoly cannot be easily broken. Over the years, the AMA's power has been blunted on occasion. President Lyndon Johnson established the Medicare and Medicaid Programs over its strong opposition. These programs provided below market prices for the elderly and the poor at the expense of the uninsured. More recently, anti-trust action by the Justice Department with potential criminal penalties has added a new dimension to action against the AMA and its members. Nevertheless, the monopoly that it helped to establish is still empowered by laws, and its insurance, industrial, and drug company allies are still able to increase profits.

From both a business and a scientific point of view, there is a simple, but not easy, solution to our problem: **Competition!** Reestablishment of medicine as a sacred art would free physicians to use effective low cost therapies forbidden by the AMA and FDA. Encouragement of competition in medical care-related industries would provide more options and lower costs for consumers. Unfortunately, the political obstacles in the way of this simple solution are enormous. The political influence of the AMA, and the web of State and Federal laws empowering it, are formidable obstacles. Even more formidable is the political influence wielded by the pharmaceutical industry, the insurance industry, and industrial lobbies.

Further institutionalization of the present system can easily result in substantially reduced availability of medical services, increased death rates, and an increasingly unhealthy population. Free competition in the medical marketplace can lower costs. Use of the advances in medical science that the monopoly has been suppressing for 100 years can increase the quality of care. However, effecting the changes necessary to permit free competition and the use of suppressed medical science will not be easy.

Nutrition is an extremely important factor in health, and affects both physical and mental health. In ancient times this truth was widely recognized, and great pains were taken to obtain proper nutrition. Unfortunately, with the modern availability of plentiful and varied foods (at least in the industrialized world) popular interest in understanding nutrition and its effects has waned. Interest in nutrition also took a nose dive when, in the 1950s, the National Academy of Sciences recommended daily allowances for food supplements and suggested that all anyone needed for good health was a balanced diet.

The amount of money being spent to keep things as they are precludes easy change. We have learned over the past 100 years that we cannot depend on our senators and representatives to eliminate the monopoly from our medical care system anytime soon. Senator Tobey's unsuccessful efforts to start a Congressional investigation of cancer research, and Senator Bricker's successful efforts to bury the Fitzgerald Report, demonstrates this point eloquently.

To eliminate the monopoly in a reasonable amount of time, "We the People" will have to work at the State level first. A state-by-state ratification of an amendment to each state constitution and ultimately the Federal Bill of Rights to ensure freedom of choice in medical care modalities for both practitioners and patients can help to reestablish competition in the medical market place. In a free marketplace, suppressing advances in medical science will be difficult, if not impossible.

CHAPTER 2 - HOMEOPATHY

At the end of the 18th century mainstream physicians were using the medical technology developed by their predecessors in more ancient times. The results they were obtaining were less than satisfactory. Their dependence on bloodletting and heavy doses of toxic remedies were making them unpopular, and the time was ripe for major change.

In America, Dr. Benjamin Rush was a leading physician and professor of medicine in the early days of the Republic. He believed that irregular arterial action was the principal cause of disease. A major internal cause was excess excitement, and that other causes were intoxicating liquors, and miasmas. External violence produced excitement. Debility was a predisposing cause of disease.

Dr. Rush's therapeutics called for stimulants to counteract debility and for other medicines to counteract the irregular arterial action resulting from the debility. Some diffusible stimulants were alcohol, opium, ether, and "volatile salts." Mixed stimulants included garlic, mercury and Peruvian bark. He recommended healthy food as a durable stimulant. Bloodletting was recommended to counteract debility even when the patient was unable to sit up without fainting. Children and infants were subjected to the same treatments as adults. To correct excessive arterial action, his arsenal included bleeding, vomiting, purges, sweats, diuretics, digitalis, niter, mercury, and lead based medicines. Thomas Jefferson, understandably, had a low opinion of American physicians.

Meanwhile in Europe, Rudolph Virchow, a German physiologist, reported that confidence in therapeutics was low, and most physicians were convinced that "no genuine therapy exists." Francoise Magendie, chair of medicine at the College de France, agreed with the French public's estimate that physicians were almost impotent to cure diseases.

In Germany, physicians were in the same boat as those in America and the rest of Europe. But one of them, Samuel Hahnemann, was so frustrated with practicing medicine "by the book" without a sound underlying theory, that he quit and began an extensive review of the literature of medicine and science. He was aided in his research by an interest in science and an unusual linguistic capability. As a child of 12 he was already fluent in English, French, Greek, and Latin, as well as his native German. This enabled him to survive by translating books and manuscripts for others.

Samuel Hahnemann was the third child and eldest son of a pottery painter who lived in Meissen, Germany. In 1775, he enrolled at the University of Leipzig's medical school eking out a meager income by translating for a fee and teaching French to a wealthy Greek. Disappointed because there was neither clinic nor hospital at the University, he transferred to Vienna in 1777, to gain clinical experience as a medical student.

Unfortunately, living in Vienna was expensive and after he was robbed, he was forced to drop out of school. However, he had impressed Professor von Quarin, physician to the royal court, who secured for him a position as physician for the Governor of Hermannstadt in Transylvania.

As family physician and curator of his patron museum and library, he catalogued the Governors coin collection, ancient books and manuscripts, and one of the finest collections of texts on alchemy and magic. He left in the spring in 1779 to register at Erlangen's medical school where he submitted a thesis on cramps. In August 1779, he registered for the degree of MD after only one term. In 1781, he became a village doctor in Mansfeld, Saxony, and in 1782, he married. Soon thereafter, in 1783, he became disenchanted with the practice of medicine and returned to translation for a fee to enhance a modest income. After a number of years of poverty and several moves, translating scientific and medical books for the Dresden Economical Society kept him occupied with a flood of orders from the scientific community. Between 1777 and 1806, he translated 24 large text books and numerous articles into German. By this means, he acquired a broad overview of scientific and medical theories and practices.

His translation of Cullen's <u>Materia Medica</u> in 1790 triggered his return to the study of medicine. Cullen believed that cinchona was a specific cure for malaria because of its tonic action on the stomach.

Hahnemann decided to investigate. He took small doses for several days and found that he experienced symptom of fever and spasms similar to malaria. This experience reminded him of an old therapeutic maxim: similia similibus curentur or 'like cures like' and stimulated him to investigate the actions of other remedies.

For years thereafter, according to reports, Hahnemann and every member of his family devoted every spare minute of their time to aspects of what he called "proving" medical remedies. They did everything from collecting herbs in the fields to assembling and numbering the symptoms observed in each person who tested remedies. In 1796, he published his *Essay on a New Principl* and resumed the practice of medicine. In 1804, he settled in Torgau, and in 1805, published Fragmenta de Viribus, a two volume work which described his new method of studying medical remedies with reports of the effects of 27 of them. His objective was to eliminate the then popular technique of dulling symptoms, and replace it with reliance on a single medicine prepared by a physician and administered in small, harmless doses to patients whose symptoms were similar to the symptoms produced by that medicine in a healthy person. His experiments with dose reductions began in 1798 and continued for the rest of his life.

A series of essays in 1805, 1808, and 1809, discussed every known mode of medical treatment and revealed why single drugs and the law of similar was superior to all of them. His <u>Organon of the Art of Healing</u> in 1810 and <u>Materia Medica Pura</u>, in 1811 provided a firm foundation for Homeopathy. In 1812, he moved back to Leipzig with the intention of taking on the allopathic medical establishment. Unfortunately, by 1820, with the antagonized medical establishment up in arms and a new governmental decree barring him from dispensing his own medicines and thus from the legal practice of homeopathy, he was force to relocate. He found a position in Coethen, governed by Duke Ferdinand, whose edict permitted Hahnemann to prepare his own medicines and practice homeopathy. He moved there in 1821, stayed for fourteen years and continued to publish books and essays. In 1928, <u>The Chronic Diseases</u> disclosed his ideas about the underlying causes of disease. It resulted in considerable controversy among his followers.

In 1835, about 5 years after the death of his first wife, he married Melanie d'Hervilly Goheir, an attractive, well connected, French artist and intellectual, 40 years younger than he, and moved to Paris. There, he established a medical practice, becoming the preferred physician of the aristocracy as well as giving free treatment to the poor. He and his wife, also expert in homeopathy, were well paid for their efforts, accumulating over four million francs before he died of bronchitis in 1843.

In his <u>Organon</u>, (1810), <u>Chronic Diseases</u>, (1828) and other writings, Hahnemann accused the allopaths of basing therapeutics on erroneous hypotheses about disease causes. In his opinion, the cause of disease was not discoverable. The germ theory of disease assumes that our bodies are sterile and microbes entering them cause disease. Koch, one of its proponents, admitted that, if disease causing bacteria were found in healthy people, the germ theory would be suspect. Healthy disease carriers and a healthy child with diphtheria bacteria in his throat were, in fact, discovered. Consequently, Hahnemann's opinion seems to have been correct, at least in his day.

Furthermore, the germ theory of disease proposed by Louis Pasteur was adopted over the objections of Claude Bernard and Antoine Bechamp. Bernard, an eminent physiologist, observed that germs are everywhere and need a receptive environment in order to cause disease. Antoine Bechamp, dean of the medical faculty at the University of Lille in France, found tiny microorganisms in cells which he called microzymas. They were pleomorphic, or could change their shape and function as their environment changed. He discovered that, after the death of the organism they inhabited, they metamorphosed into molds capable of disposing of organic matter. Microbes that could change from one form into another were a serious threat to the credibility of medical theories.

To avoid observing pleomorphic changes, allopathic physicians make sure that bacteria are dead before looking at them under the microscope. It is also notable that people who invent and use powerful microscopes are not popular. Royal Raymond Rife, who observed pleomorphic changes with his universal microscope at 50,000 times magnification, was persecuted by the AMA. Ultimately, his laboratory, notebooks, and photographic evidence of his findings, were destroyed in a mysterious break-in and fire. Gaston Naessens, a Frenchman who developed another powerful microscope, and observed pleomorphism, was prosecuted by the medical establishments in both France and Canada. This record indicates that the medical establishment may be more interested in maintaining the status quo than in advancing medical science.

Hahnemann believed Edward Jenner's cowpox inoculations to prevent smallpox infections were good examples of the law of similars. Smallpox is prevented by inoculation with a similar disease cowpox.

In 1825, homeopathy arrived in the United States and soon there was an influx of homeopathic physicians trained in Germany who came with the flood of German immigrants. Homeopathic schools were established and homeopathy began to attract attention.

The 1830's epidemics of Asiatic cholera in both France and the US tested the capabilities of both orthodox and homeopathic physicians and established the reputations of the homeopaths in both countries. The crowned heads and aristocracy in Europe and the aristocrats and plutocrats in America began to patronize homeopaths. The allopaths didn't like the competition. Members of the French Academy of

Medicine called homeopaths quacks, frauds and charlatans. American allopaths said that the excellent cure rates achieved by homeopaths were the result of treating easy cases of cholera.

American homeopaths repeated their performance during a subsequent yellow fever epidemic in the Mississippi valley in 1878, which originated in New Orleans. The 27,000 cases in New Orleans resulted in 4,600 deaths, but only 110 deaths occurred in the 1945 cases treated by homeopathic physicians. One of them was awarded a gold medal by the French government for his work during the epidemic.

Another function performed by the homeopaths was counteracting the effects of overdoses of medications in patients treated by allopaths. Large doses of quinine, mercury, and lead compounds poisoned their patients, who frequently turned to homeopathic help. Homeopathic doses of the medications that caused the problems relieved the poisoned patients. In the words of George Bernard Shaw: "the drug that gives you a headache will also cure a headache if you take little enough of it."

In the 1830's and 40's, quinine was the remedy for any fever. One ton of it was prescribed in a 10 day period in Boston. In 1844, the French Academy of Medicine warned that quinine was capable of producing serious symptoms, illness, and death. In 1847, the Medical Gazette reported that deafness, blindness, haematuria, gastritis, delirium, epilepsy, palsy, and death had been caused by quinine. In 1890, the *JAMA* noted that insufficient attention was being given to the toxic effects of quinine. Allopaths were unwilling to admit the morbidic potential of quinine, and of mercury, because this implied recognition of Hahnemann's Law of Similars. Overdoses of medications made allopaths unpopular and the homeopaths benefited.

In free competition, Americans preferred the milder homeopathic therapies to the harsher bleeding, purging, and overdosing of allopathic physicians. At the end of the 19th century there were about 15,000 relatively prosperous homeopathic physicians earning a few thousand dollars a years and 100,000 allopathic physicians averaging about $750 per year. John D. Rockefeller was a homoeopathist and Boston was a hotbed of homeopathy.

By 1892, homeopaths were operating 110 hospitals, 145 dispensaries, 62 asylums and old people's homes, 30 nursing homes and sanitaria, and 16 insane asylums. In 1889, the Westborough, Massachusetts insane asylum was operated by homeopaths and the Springfield Republican reported that the cost of maintenance was much less, and recoveries and general success greater, than in allopathic asylums.

Some insurance companies offered reduced rates to people who patronized homeopathic physicians and homeopathic life insurance companies were chartered. In 1870, Homeopathic Life of New York reported that it had sold 7,927 policies to followers of homeopathy, and 2,258 to others. Deaths numbering 84 for the first category and 66 for the second justified the lower premium to homoeopathists.

At the turn of the century, feeling secure, the homeopaths gave little support to their medical society. They didn't realize that George Simmons, MD, the new editor of *JAMA*, who had graduated from a homeopathic college, was plotting their downfall. It did not take long for their reputation for superior performance in cholera and yellow fever epidemics and excellent service in the last 75 years of the 19th century to be forgotten, as hundreds of millions of dollars were spent establishing a monopoly, under the banner of "scientific medicine," whose first objective was to raise the status and income of allopathic physicians.

George Bernard Shaw noted in the preface to his play "The Doctor's Dilemma" published in 1907, that "the savage opposition which homeopathy encountered from the medical profession was not a scientific opposition; for nobody seems to deny that some drugs act in the alleged manner. It was opposed simply because doctors and apothecaries lived by selling bottles and boxes of doctor's stuff to be taken by the spoonfuls or in pellets as large as peas; and people would not pay as much for drops and globules no larger than pins' heads."

The AMA's campaign, under the direction of Simmons and his successor Morris Fishbein, MD, discredited the homeopaths. Fishbein had poor grades in medical school and never practiced medicine but promoted himself to be an expert on every aspect of it. He organized the AMA's public relations campaign which did not hesitate to denigrate competitors. He also helped the AMA convince the Association of Science Writers that, as a matter of policy, they should check with medical and scientific experts before publishing any new discoveries. When newspaper editors adopted the same policy, it was almost impossible for the public to hear "the other side of the story."

Today, homeopathy is making a comeback. Some say homoeopathists are increasing in numbers at the rate of 20% per year, but homeopathic physicians are not so easy to find. There is no homeopathic physician listed in the yellow pages of the North Country telephone book.

CHAPTER 3 - HEART DISEASE

In 2005, the American Heart Association estimated that 63 million Americans suffered from cardiovascular disease and more than one million had heart operations. The Milken Institute estimated direct costs for treatment of this disease were $65 billion, and lost economic output another $105 billion, in 2003, with an expected increase of 41% by 2023 because of our aging population. Actual costs totaled $156 billion in 2009 according to the American Heart Association. But while costs are expected to increase, death rates have been decreasing for the last 20 years.

According to the Census Bureau's Statistical Abstract of the United States, major cardiovascular diseases killed 1 million Americans in 1970 but only 916,000 in 1990. Heart disease deaths declined from 736,000 to 720,000 in the same period. The decline has continued. There were 652,000 heart disease deaths in 2005, and 616,000 in 2007. In 1970, age adjusted deaths per 100,000 were 559, and declined to 211 per 100,000 in 2005. Deaths from atherosclerosis were only 32,000 in 1970, and reached 18,000 in 1990. If these trends continue, heart disease, as number 1 killer of Americans, may lose its place to Cancer.

Substantial reduction in costs of treating heart disease can be obtained quickly and easily by utilizing unexploited discoveries of medical scientists suppressed by the medical monopoly. Judicious use of vitamin C, and the essential amino acid lysine, vitamin E, and chelation therapy with ethelenediaminetetraaceticacid (EDTA) can make a big dent in the costs of treating heart disease.

A campaign to discourage use of dietary supplements began in the 1950's. The Research Council of the National Academy of Sciences established recommended daily allowances (RDA's) of vitamins and minerals which were minimum requirements to avoid deficiency diseases in otherwise perfectly healthy young adults. Few realize that they don't apply to anyone over forty. The medical establishment declared that these, and a balanced diet, were all anyone needed for good health. Furthermore, the FDA began a series of attempts to make more than the RDA amounts of supplements available only with a physician's prescription. They would like to turn dietary supplements into drugs.

Long ago scientists noticed that the majority of wild animals do not get heart attacks or cardiovascular disease. They also found that most of them make their own vitamin C, or ascorbic acid, and that goats are particularly good at this. Under stress, some of them can make 100 grams of it in a day. However, the guinea pig, which is unable to make its own ascorbate, does get cardiovascular disease. Research indicates that only those animals which do not make their own vitamin C internally are susceptible to heart attacks and cardiovascular disease. These few include a fruit eating bat, the guinea pig, and the primates. Humans also lack this capability. Vitamin C, which exists in our bodies as ascorbates, is an orthomolecular (right molecule) substance our bodies used to be able to make internally. Our ancestors are believed to have lost the capability about 20 million years ago.

Heart disease is believed to begin with atherosclerosis, plaque, or scab formation, inside our arteries. Plaque forms as a result of damage, either caused mechanically or due to attack by free radicals. The process starts with the formation of an atheroma, a little tumor, with no blood supply of its own. As it grows, its interior deteriorates, because diffusion of oxygen and nutrients through the thickening walls becomes inadequate. In the final stages, the deteriorated regions fill with cholesterol and calcium. Furthermore, oxidized cholesterol acts like vitamin D and assists in the hardening process.

Pioneering research, begun in the late 1940's in Canada by Dr. G. C. Willis, proved that vitamin C deficiency caused atherosclerosis. Canadian physicians found that 100% of animals, which do not make their own vitamin C internally, develop the disease when deprived of the vitamin. They also proved that vitamin C reversed atherosclerosis in laboratory animals [14]. These experimental results clearly indicate that

---

14 G. C. Willis, *The Reversibility of Atherosclerosis*, "Canadian Medical Association Journal," V77, 106-109, July 15 1957.

atherosclerosis is an aspect of the dietary deficiency disease scurvy.

Early studies showed that atherosclerotic plaques could be reversed in human patients. Low doses of vitamin C, about 1500 milligrams/day (mg/d), reversed plaques in 1/3 of patients. [15]. This important finding has been suppressed for many years. Meanwhile, patients have been told, and some are still being told, that taking more than the recommended daily allowance of vitamin C, 60 mg/day, only produced expensive urine.

Linus Pauling and Matteus Rath confirmed the Canadian findings in the 1980s [16]. Their paper on this subject, which identified atherosclerosis as pre scurvy, was accepted for publication by the Proceedings of the National Academy of Sciences – and then rejected. This was the first rejection of a paper submitted by a member of the Academy. (Some suspect the rejection was effected by AMA members in the Academy.) Their paper was published subsequently in the Journal of Orthomolecular Medicine which MEDLINE, a primary source of information for American physicians, has refused to abstract for over 35 years. Additional papers describing successful use of vitamin C and lysine in

---

15 G. C. Will et al, *Serial Autobiography in Atherosclerosis*, "Canadian Medical Association Journal," V 71, 562-8, December 1964.
16 Rath, M. and Pauling, L., *Solution to the Puzzle of Human Cardiovascular Disease*, "Journal of Orthomolecular Medicine" 6, 125-134.

heart disease cases [17,18] were also published in the JOM. These facts indicate that an inadequate supply of vitamin C is an important risk factor for heart disease.

In 1992, Dr. Pauling recorded a lecture explaining his hypothesis and disclosing his discovery of a rapid cure for atherosclerosis using vitamin C and lysine. (It should be noted that vitamin C, the essential amino acid lysine and proline, which we make internally, are required for the formation of collagen which holds our bodies together.) Owen R. Fonorow acquired the rights to Pauling's lecture on vitamin C and heart disease in his company Intelisoft Multimedia, Inc., and has attempted to promote it. Tower Laboratories Corporation has also been promoting a product with the high doses of lysine and vitamin C that Pauling found to be effective. (2 to 6 grams/day of lysine and 6 to 18 grams/day of vitamin C). Mattias Rath also promotes products using this technology.

In 1998, and again in 2001, the Vitamin C Foundation requested grants from the Office of Alternative Medicine at the National Institutes of Health to investigate the applicability of Pauling's theory to human subjects. Both requests were refused. It is notable that the NIH itself failed to initiate any studies of its own to explore Pauling's theory.

---

17 Pauling, L., *Case Report on Lysine/Ascorbate related amelioration of Angina Pectoris*, "Journal of Orthomolecular Medicine" 6:144-146.
18 Pauling L., *Case Report on Lysine-Ascorbate amelioration of Angina Pectoris*. "Journal of Orthomolecular Medicine" 8:137-138.

The January-February 2009 issue of Nexus New Times carries an interesting article on Scurvy and Heart Disease by Owen R. Fonorow. He reports that no one, with the exception of Linus Pauling and Mattias Rath, has replicated the early work on vitamin C and heart disease in the last 50 years. This is a notable failure of a medical establishment that claims that it is practicing "Scientific Medicine." It is reasonable to believe that this failure has cost the people of the United States billions of dollars and immense amounts of sickness and suffering. The American public remains uninformed about this discovery, and most American cardiologists do not use the simple, inexpensive therapy that Pauling prescribed.

Thomas Levy, MD, JD, believes that the origin of all cardiovascular disease is a reversible deficiency of inexpensive vitamin C. His book Stop America's #1 Killer, with over 60 pages of references, provides the basis for upgrading the Pauling-Rath hypothesis to the status of theory. Furthermore, his data indicates that adequate amounts of vitamin C can not only protect us against heart disease, but improve our health, and extend our lives.

When insufficient amounts of ascorbate are circulating in our blood streams, the connective tissues in the walls of our arteries lose strength and become mushy and watery. This permits penetration by LDL and other substances which ultimately results in plaque deposits. Levy provides reasons for believing that elevated cholesterol and high blood pressure are not the primary culprits in cardiovascular disease.

In a foreword to the book, Dr. Julian Whittaker, suggests that the discovery and utilization of vitamins and minerals, orthomolecular substances, in the prevention and treatment of diseases is the greatest medical advancement of the 20th century. He notes that most prescription drugs, with the exception of some hormones, are not found in our bodies and are foreign to life. However, due to yearly expenditures of $16 billion on direct-to-physician promotion of drugs and another $4 billion on consumer advertising, the use of orthomolecular substances has been forgotten and is generally scorned by the medical profession.

The last chapter of the book provides detailed information about stopping and reversing atherosclerosis. The first recommendation is to eliminate dental toxicity from mercury amalgam fillings and root canals. Next follows a number of food related recommendations based on an earlier book Optimal Nutrition for Optimal Health. The final section contains a recommended list of dietary supplements. Heart disease patients will find this book interesting and informative. The information in it may help them live longer and feel better.

Conventional medical treatments for various aspects of heart disease employ drugs which deal with symptoms. Many cause collateral damage. For example, cholesterol lowering statin drugs, which reduce production of cholesterol in the liver, also reduce the liver's production of co-enzyme Q-10. This reduces energy production in all cells, including heart cells, and weakens the heart. Some drugs may even cause, as side effects, the very symptoms being treated. For example, some drugs for atrial fibrillation can cause it. Heart disease is big business.

Our laws supporting the medical monopoly hinder the dissemination of information about the usefulness of un-patentable products like vitamin C without the expenditure of millions of dollars for, in this case, clearly unnecessary tests to prove safety and efficacy. Therefore, only a small number of people have benefited from knowledge of Dr. Pauling pre-scurvy theory. For example, one of my personal friends, who had a clogged carotid artery, added six grams per day of lysine to the eight grams of vitamin C she took daily and her clogged carotid artery cleared in a couple of months.

Recent research in England has made it easier to evaluate the condition of arteries in our bodies. The plaques that clog arteries around the heart also appear, on a smaller scale, in the eyes. Dr. Sidney Bush, DOpt at the Hull Contact Lens and Eye Clinic in England accidentally discovered that they could be reversed. During an investigation of eye infections in contact lens wearers, he found that "soft" atheromas disappeared in patients taking 3,000 to 10,000 mg/d of vitamin C. He subsequently discovered that even "hard" atheromas can be made to disappear after two years.

Dr. Bush has invented a procedure called CardioRetinometry to diagnose atherosclerosis simply and easily by evaluation of conditions in the eyes of patients. Dr. Bush believes that eye doctors can easily diagnose chronic scurvy by microscopic examination of arteries behind the eyes even before symptoms of heart disease appear.

The United Nation's Codex Alimentarious recommends a daily allowance of 60 mg/d of vitamin C with a maximum tolerable allowance of 2000 mg/d and limits the amount of this vitamin that consumers can buy without a prescription. It is already in force in several countries. Our membership in the International Trade Organization requires us to incorporate its provisions in our law. Bills to incorporate it into our laws are periodically introduced in Congress. Are they designed to insure the continuation of heart disease as a major source of income for the medical-industrial monopoly? If the Codex restrictions are made to apply in the United States, all Americans, not just heart disease patients, will suffer irreparable harm.

Also notable is the fact that vitamin C is no longer manufactured in the United States. Well over 90% of what we use is imported from China. The consequences of an interruption of supply of this essential material could be catastrophic. Reestablishing domestic manufacturing capacity warrants a high priority.

HEART SURGERY – COSMETIC CARDIOLOGY?

Dr. Bruce West, in his Health Alert letter of June 2010 estimates that $100 billion of health care costs could be saved in one year by eliminating interventional cardiology. This kind of surgery invades over 1 million American hearts a year in efforts to alleviate the effects of clogged arteries.

Heart surgery to improve circulation began in the 1950s. An early procedure involved placing a sac around the heart with a powder inside to improve nutrition and oxygenation. This was called pericardial poundrage. It didn't work. Then tying off the clogged artery in hopes of increasing collateral circulation was tried. This didn't work either. Next, the coronary artery bypass graft was developed. Ten years of experience showed that half the patients who received it had a rough time recovering. Many suffered memory loss and some became invalids. However, 65% of bypass patients were alive after 5 years while only 45% of patients who received sham surgeries survived that long.

Subsequently, balloon angioplasty was developed. A balloon was inserted into a clogged artery and inflated in the area of the clog in the hope of expanding the artery and spreading the plaque. A friend who was a professor of internal medicine at Georgetown University underwent this procedure and died 6 months later. This technique was discarded because it was no more successful than the bypass operation, and arteries tended to clog up again.

The next development was the stent, a wire tube placed in the area where the balloon had expanded the plaque to prevent subsequent collapse. This didn't work, nor did stents covered with drugs designed to keep arteries open according to Dr. West. Another friend, who had been taking large amounts of vitamin E, underwent the procedure and wound up with seven holes in her skull, and on a breathing machine for several weeks because of bleeding and herniation of her brain. She spent months recovering in a nursing home and never returned to normal activities. The surgeon knew in advance of the vitamin E intake.

Plaque and clogs can cause impaired coronary artery circulation, angina, stroke, and even death. However, most plaque is slow growing and your body can develop collateral circulation, new blood vessels that bypass the clog. Pigs have been able, with proper nutrition, to develop adequate collateral circulation in 6 to 8 weeks. Humans can do it in 4 to 12 months also, with proper nutritional support.

Incidentally, Dr. West believes that meaningful health care reform will never happen because of the economic impact of unemployment of health care workers and the obsolescence of health care and medical industrial facilities. In other words, in his opinion, the medical-industrial establishment is too big and important to fail!

VITAMIN E AND HEART DISEASE

Discovered in 1922, vitamin E was first identified as the fertility vitamin. It was not until 1945 that the Canadians, Evan and Wilfred Schute, began a serious investigation of its other uses. Vitamin E by Herbert Baley contains much information about the vitamin and Evan Schute, a genius who entered college at the age of 14, quickly found that the vitamin was useful in the treatment of heart disease. Alpha Tocopherol in Cardiovascular Disease, published in 1954 disclosed the results of treating more than 10,000 cardiac patients with vitamin E. The book was published because medical journals refused to publish their groundbreaking investigations of vitamin E. Nor would the National Research Council of Canada register their manuscript. The medical establishment was not willing to accept their work without the expensive double blind studies which prevent easy acceptance of medical innovation. The Schutes were unwilling to deprive any patient of this valuable vitamin so there was an impasse.

Nevertheless, research continued, and the Schute Foundation for Medical Research was formed. Over 80,000 cardiac patients were treated successfully between 1954 and 1993. Most heart specialists condemned the vitamin therapy at first sight. Over the years, resistance diminished and physicians began taking vitamin E and some of them even prescribed it for their patients. The good news about vitamin E finally got to the public.

In early 1975 Richard Passwater published the results of a survey of almost 18,000 readers of Prevention Magazine which indicated that those who took 400 international units of vitamin E or more for long periods of time substantially reduced their risk of heart attacks. Those who took these amounts for 10 years prior to reaching the age of 80 reduced their risk of heart attacks by 90%. Those who took these amounts for 4 years prior to 80 reduced their risk by about 65%.

In 1993, studies sponsored by Harvard Medical School resulted in the finding that heart attack risk was reduced by 40% for those who took 100 IU or more of vitamin E for 4 to 10 years as compared with those who received all their vitamin E from food.

The Schute Institute recommended that patients with hypertensive heart disease start with 400 IU of vitamin E per day for 4 weeks, 800 IU per day for an additional 4 weeks and cautious increase in dosage. Hypertensive agents are needed along with the vitamin E. Other varieties of heart disease were treated with 800 to 2400 IU of vitamin E per day.

CHELATION THERAPY

After World War II, many naval shipyard workers were suffering from lead poisoning because of the extensive use of lead based paint as primers for metal surfaces. Lead poisoning is very debilitating and many of these workers were in poor condition. Enterprising physicians decided to try removing the lead from the bodies of these workers with a chelating agent, ethylenediaminetetraaceticacid (EDTA). EDTA has a molecular structure which looks something like a cup formed by 4 acid radicals. It is able to sequester metal ions in this cup and carry them out of the body through the kidneys. A number of different metal ions can be removed from the blood stream with EDTA including iron, copper, calcium, and lead.

The chelation experiment worked as expected to remove the lead, but there were unexpected benefits. Those treated not only lost the symptoms of lead poisoning, but of several other diseases including cardiovascular disease (CVD). Clogged arteries were unclogged, angina disappeared, and the cost of the treatments, 30 sessions at about $100 per session, was low in relation to heart surgery which could cost $50,000.

Early on, the removal of calcium "rivets" holding plaque to the walls of arteries was believed to be the mechanism by which chelation helped people with CVD. The mechanism is now known to be far more sophisticated. Less than one-half of a gram of ionic calcium removed from the bloodstream during chelation treatment lowers its concentration and triggers a response from the parathyroid gland. The gland sends out its messenger, a parahormone, which tells body systems to scavenge calcium from storage to replace the amount removed. The most available calcium is in the plaque! Also, providentially, this hormone stimulates the bones to put more bone building into operation to protect the skeleton. The bone-building effect is said to continue for three months and results in stronger bones.

So how does chelation get rid of the plaque? The simple, perhaps incredible, answer seems to be that it clears out the heavy metals and copper and iron, which poison the body. The body then can heal itself. That is, if the proper nutrients are supplied in adequate quantities, and care is taken to minimize the introduction of more of the poison that caused the problem. Furthermore, since these same enzyme poisons are responsible for a lot of other malfunctions, this one treatment can logically be expected to have manifold benefits. And it does.

Investigators in other countries also found that chelation can provide another unexpected benefit. More than 20 years ago scientists in Switzerland from the Institute for Radiation Therapy and Nuclear Medicine at the University of Zurich discovered that chelation therapy substantially reduced cancer death rates among Swiss citizens exposed to lead from automobile exhausts. Aware of the importance of this discovery and the controversy that might arise because of it, Drs. W. Blumer and T. Reich submitted their data to a skeptical epidemiologist for review. He could find nothing wrong, so they published their findings in a 1980 issue of Environmental International.

Their paper disclosed that only 1 of 59 people who had received chelation therapy died of cancer during their 18 years of monitoring the group exposed to high traffic. In comparison, 30 of the 172 people who did not receive chelation – the rest of the 231 people with high traffic exposure – died during the same period. Clearly chelation therapy had reduced cancer risk by more than 90% in this experiment. Deaths from all causes were also lower among these fortunate Swiss.

Dr. Bruce Halstead, author of The Scientific Basis of Chelation Therapy suggests that reduction in levels of free radicals resulting from the removal of iron, copper, lead, and other heavy metals from the bloodstream is responsible for the major benefits of this therapy. The Swiss experience indicates that the effects are lasting.

Nevertheless, the AMA considers chelation therapy for the treatment of arteriosclerosis and related disorders as useless "because the effects are not long lasting." This opinion was issued in 1966. In 1976, the California Medical Association Council echoed the AMA's opinion, saying: "The efficacy of chelation therapy in the treatment of arteriosclerosis is not proven and is not now an accepted therapy." The following year, the California Department of Health and the Board of Medical Quality Assurance attempted to prevent physicians from using EDTA for chelation by threatening criminal prosecution. They were frustrated, however, by the California attorney general. In 1978, the FDA attempted to obtain an injunction against Dr. H.R.

Evers who was giving chelation treatments in Alabama. In the case brought against Evers, FDA officials argued that there was a strong medical school of thought that chelation had not been clinically proven. But the weight of evidence submitted was to the contrary, and the court ruled against the FDA.

In another case, a Federal Trade Commission judge determined that the AMA had produced a formidable impediment to competition in the delivery of medical care services to physicians in this country. "That barrier has served to deprive consumers of the free flow of information about the availability of health care services, to deter the offering of innovative forms of medical care, and to stifle the rise of almost every type of medical care delivery that could potentially pose a threat to the income of fee-for-service physicians in private practice," said the court.

Daniel Haley, in his remarkably informative book Politics in Healing, notes that the Berkeley, Harvard, and Mayo Clinic newsletters condemned chelation therapy in 2000.

To insist that a procedure is unproven, which has benefited millions of people with fewer than 30 deaths reported, flies in the face of reason. Especially since the US Office of Technology Assessment, a Congressional watchdog agency, has determined that only 10 to 20% of procedures currently used in medical practice have been shown to be efficacious by controlled trials. Nevertheless, in 1998, the FTC took ACAM to court based on a brochure's statement that

77

chelation is an effective treatment for CVD. Since ACAM did not have the two double-blind, placebo-controlled studies to support this claim, the FTC asked the court to place ACAM on probation for 20 years.

It should be evident from the above discussion that, scientific research already accomplished and paid for, can extend the useful lives of Americans with heart disease and reduce the cost of care. The principal impediment to use of this research is our medical monopoly. It has been opposing applications of advancements in medical science that promised to reduce costs and improve quality of medical services for 100 years.

CHAPTER 4 - CANCER

Cancer is an ancient disease. There is evidence that it even plagued dinosaurs. Hippocrates of Cos treated cancer in ancient Greece. Healers of every culture have struggled with it, and some treatments have been in use for over 2500 years. North American Indian shamans were curing cancer long before European colonists arrived and American physicians learned how to use their knowledge. There were even some American physicians who were curing a high percentage of their cancer patients a hundred and fifty years ago.

The War on Cancer began in 1971, during the Nixon Administration, and has seen countless billions of dollars 'invested' in cancer research with little significant progress toward winning the war. All this research has resulted in increasingly expensive therapies - surgery, radiation, chemotherapy - but cure rates have remained abysmally low. The treatments offered by the medical establishment as its standards of practice, maim, burn, and damage patients at great expense, while faster, gentler, and less expensive therapies have been actively suppressed by the allopathic medical monopoly for many years.

A critical assessment of the history of the war on cancer indicates that the major beneficiaries have not been cancer patients. After several decades of steady increases, the US cancer death rate stabilized from 1990 to 1992 and has then declined slightly from 1992 to 2006. Costs of treatment, however, have steadily risen. The war effort has provided well-paid employment for many physicians, a basic objective of the AMA, and a bonanza for pharmaceutical companies, research laboratories, and fund-raising organizations. To keep the gravy train rolling, the AMA, in conjunction with its allies in industry and government, has consistently suppressed advances in medical science and technology which could have provided life-saving remedies to cancer patients, and insights into the answers to many of the questions that still have no officially sanctioned answers.

There are reasons to believe that the concept of cancer as a local disease that metastasizes is flawed. Dr. Otto Warburg's discovery that cancer results when cells are deprived of oxygen, for which he won a Nobel Prize, supports the theory that cancer is a systemic disease with local manifestations. If it *is* a systemic disease, then the destruction of the immune systems of cancer patients through chemotherapy is counterproductive.

No one has yet definitively identified why people develop cancer. The best that has been done so far is to identify "risk factors," and certain of those factors, like smoking, have received wide publicity while others have not. The National Cancer Institute (part of the NIH) helpfully identifies a major risk factor for us - growing older! It admits that "doctors often cannot explain why one person develops cancer and another does not."

One potentially important initiator of cancer (and possibly other diseases) is a type of unidentified radiation from within the earth. This radiation is concentrated in narrow areas by both geological structures and rapidly flowing underground streams of water. European studies in several countries leave little doubt that such dangerous radiation exists. An investigation in Vermont a number of years ago showed that it is also present in the United States. Because establishment science is unable to explain this radiation, it maintains that it doesn't exist and ignores an important hazard to health and welfare. The radiation is detectable both with electronic equipment and by competent and experienced dowsers.

There has been a broad and strenuous resistance in the medical profession against un-sanctioned research, independent investigation, and free-thinking practitioners of the healing arts. While not every claim can be verified, and not every "cure" is real, it is worse than irresponsible to simply reject out-of-hand any discovery or methodology that shows promise just because it does not have the prior approval of the American Medical Association. Viable treatments for cancer have been suppressed and the lack of progress has been used as a justification for continuing the War on Cancer.

THE WAR ON CANCER

In the 1920's tuberculosis (TB) was the number two killer of Americans and research efforts were directed at finding a cure for TB, and for venereal diseases. Harry Hoxsey notes in his 1956 book You Don't Have to Die that science, with the aid of magic bullets, conquered both of these plagues, but science failed to cope with cancer, the third leading cause of death. During the 30 years prior to 1956, cancer deaths more than doubled in nearly every civilized nation of the world. Cancer took TB's place as the second leading cause of death. About 250,000 American were being

81

killed by cancer every year in the 1950's. In 1972, about 1,500,000 Americans had cancer, and 350,000 died of it.

At the start of the War on Cancer, in 1971, the Internet edition of Statistical Abstract of the United States reports that the age adjusted death rate for cancer (malignant neoplasms) was 199 per 100,000, up from 194 per 100,000 in 1960. After almost 20 years of warfare, in 1990 the age adjusted death rate per 100,000 increased to 216 an 8% increase. In 2005, after 34 years of war, the death rate per 100,000 was 184 – an approximate 6% reduction from 1971. Is this a stalemate?

The cost of treating American cancer patients has been about 4.5% of total medical care costs for 40 years. It was $78 billion in 2007. About 500,000 American cancer patients are dying every year. The American Cancer Society estimated that 562,000 died of the disease in 2009. The people, who have supported this war with their charitable contributions and tax dollars, have not been well served. A review of the strategy and tactics being used in the conduct of this war is long overdue.

The strategy is based on the theory that cancer originates as a local disease (of the breast or prostate gland for example) and then metastasizes to other parts of the body. The tactics used involve surgical removal of as much cancerous tissue as possible as soon as possible after discovery, followed by X-ray or radium treatments and/or chemotherapy to prevent or limit or destroy metastases.

The theory that cancer starts as a local disease is an off-shoot of Pasteur's germ theory of disease. There is a high probability that it is not correct. Substantial evidence shows that cancer is a systemic disease.

Physicians and scientists who have treated cancer as a systemic disease have met with considerable success. Unfortunately, they have not been applauded and copied by mainstream medicine. Rather, they have been consistently denigrated and persecuted for almost a century, and American patients have suffered as a result.

Antoine Bechamp, dean of the medical faculty at the University of Lille, challenged Pasteur's germ theory at its inception. Although his obituary, published in a scientific journal, took 8 pages to list his honors and scientific achievements, records of his existence are hard to find. His admirers in France are attempting to correct this deficiency.

Bechamp discovered almost invisible micro-organisms with enzymatic activity in blood and tissue, which he called microzymas, tiny ferments. His research determined that they were practically indestructible, withstanding both chemical attack and temperatures in excess of 200° C. He also found that they were pleomorphic, capable of changing their shape and size. Furthermore, he found that they were capable of changing into forms capable of causing both disease and the final dissolution of tissues. Bechamp's work indicated that the internal condition of the body was critically important and that disease could occur because of the actions of the microzymas in the absence of other causes. Claude Bernard, an eminent French physiologist, also considered that the environment inside the body is critically important for the development of disease. It has been reported that Pasteur, on his deathbed, said: "Bernard was right, the milieu is everything, and the bacteria is nothing!"

Guenther Enderline, a German zoologist,

83

continued Bechamp's research and found that the microzymas, which he renamed protits, could develop into cancer causing organisms. In fact, he developed Isopathic therapies for treating cancer and other diseases which used protits, or combinations of them, to "mate" with the more complex disease causing forms and destroy them.

Pasteur's followers, and medical establishments in many countries, have ignored and suppressed Bechamp's and Enderlein's discoveries, and the research supporting their concepts. Nevertheless, a substantial body of sound, scientifically based research has developed. The peer review process has effectively kept most of this work out of the orthodox literature, but evidence of it is available for those who wish to look. And those who do look can find alternative strategies based on the conclusion that cancer is a systematic disease.

Our War on Cancer has been amply financed with billions of dollars of Government funds and private contributions. Unfortunately, during almost 40 years of expensive research and development, little has been accomplished by the army of physicians and scientists employed in this activity. The American Cancer Society reported the first decrease in total annual cancer deaths occurred in 2003 – 369 or less than 0.1%. Another decrease of 3,014 followed in 2004. This amounts to a total decrease of about 0.6% for the two years. Hardly an impressive achievement, when 553,888 patients died in 2004 and 562,000 in 2009.

From time to time, serious questions have been raised by concerned investigators. In 1986, Dr. John C. Bailar of Harvard Medical School and Dr. Elaine Smith of University of Iowa Medical Center published their review of progress against cancer in the *New England Journal of Medicine*. They found that overall cancer death rates had increased by 8.5% between 1950 and 1982, a period of unprecedented expenditures on research and clinical investigations. The Office concluded that: "We are losing the war against cancer" since there was little or no improvement in patient survival rates for the 12 most common cancers from 1950 to 1982 despite the expenditure of $1 billion a year on US cancer research. Also, in 1987, Dr. Samuel Epstein of the University of Illinois Medical Center, in a statement in the Congressional Record, said that Congress had not recognized that we were losing the war against cancer. In 2004, Representative Henry Waxman, ranking minority member of the Committee on Government Reform said, "Over the past several decades, while rates of heart disease have dropped dramatically, rates of cancer have largely remained stable… cancer will still kill an estimated 500,000 Americans in 2004."

We are not alone in spending a great deal of public money on medical research with unimpressive results. Richard Milton's Forbidden Science, published in Great Britain in 1994, reports that 20 years of British medical research, costing about two billion pounds (at 1993 prices), did not make a big difference in the incidence of disease and death in that country. He notes that life expectancy at 45 had hardly changed since the beginning of the century.

Unfortunately for cancer patients, and taxpayers, too, a number of talented people discovered effective cancer treatments but they were suppressed by a medical establishment intent on maintaining control of the practice of medicine. Daniel Haley, a former member of the New York Legislature, published a book

85

in 2000, <u>Politics in Healing</u>, which documents the trials and tribulations of a number of these innovators.

A 2,500 YEAR OLD TREATMENT FOR CANCER

Escharotic treatment of cancer has been in continuous use for over 2,500 years. Escharotic means scar forming; a caustic substance capable of producing a slough, a mass of dead tissue that eventually separates and falls away from the body. The medications may be acids or bases. Treatments with botanicals have earned the respect of both patients and practitioners. They were still popular in rural areas of the Carolinas, Tennessee, Oklahoma, and the Rocky Mountains, in 1999 according to Ingrid Naiman who wrote <u>Cancer Salves</u>, published by the 7th Ray Press. These treatments are less painful and less invasive than surgery and chemotherapy according to Naiman, but they are not pleasant, nor do they offer assurance that death will be forestalled.

There are three basic types of these herbal salves: (1) causes chemical action producing heat that destroys tumors; (2) causes chemical reactions that necrotize tumors on contact with or without production of heat; (3) stimulates circulation by oxygenating healthy tissue thereby promoting tumor separation. A number of practitioners and physicians have published books and papers about their experiences with these herbal treatments, among them are:

Hildegard of Bingen, Germany, a mystic and healer in 800 AD, wrote about "vermes" dying when they tasted her cancer salve which included violets and

Billy-Goat Tallow.

Dr. Weldon Fell, an American physician developed a highly successful cancer treatment based on bloodroot sap, used by American Indians in the Lake Superior region to treat cancer. He was a member of the faculty of New York University and helped found the New York Academy of Medicine. He also worked at Middlesex hospital in Great Britain. He published a study in 1858 which revealed that 8 of 10 surgical patients treated for cancer returned for further treatment within 2 years, whereas only 3 of 10 treated with bloodroot paste had a recurrence of cancer in 2 years.

Dr. Richard Guy of London, England, described 100 cancer cases treated with a poultice.

Dr. Eli Jones, an American physician reported on treating over 20,000 patients, taught other physicians how to treat cancers and disclosed composition of his medications. He cured his first cancer patient in 1869.

Dr. Frederick E. Mohs, an American physician and graduate of the University of Wisconsin Medical School, published a book, Chemosurgery in Cancer, Gangrene and Infections, providing 5 year survival rates of 9,716 cases of basal cell carcinoma and 3,299 cases of squamous cell carcinoma of the skin.

Harry Hoxsey, an American medical entrepreneur, described his experience with cancer therapy in his book You Don't Have to Die, published in 1956. His technology was similar to Mohs', except that Hoxsey used secret formulas developed by his grandfather. Hoxsey ran the largest chain of cancer clinics in history with affiliates in 17 states. His Texas clinic was said to be the largest in the world.

ESCAROTIC SALVES USED IN THE US
BEFORE 1900

Dr. John Pattison introduced the use of American herbal alkaloids to British physicians. He opposed the use of arsenic preparations such as those popularized by Justamond in the 17th century and later by Girouard. He also objected to the use of pure ZnCl2 (zinc chloride) because of the intolerable pain it caused. He used ZnCl2 with goldenseal which both reduced pain and the risk of recurrence, increasing concentration of ZnCl2 as treatment progressed and sensitivity to pain decreased. For deep tumors he used HNO3 (nitric acid) of specific gravity 1.35, rubbing it into the skin over the tumor. For 1 week he gradually increased the concentration of his enucleating agent composed of goldenseal root, ZnCl2, flour and H2O in calendula ointment. Then he started scoring the eschar with a sharp instrument and treating the scores with enucleating paste. Tumors died gradually in 14 to 21 days. After he removed them, he inspected the sites for possible remaining cancer tissue, treating it with a weak enucleating paste. Final treatment varied with the appearance of the site. Hot water infusions of poke root might be applied. The wounds were said to heal in 3 to 4 weeks after removal of the dead tumor. He estimated his recurrence rate was 15%. However, only about 10% of his patients received enucleation treatments since he considered them an aid and not a cure. He used homeopathic preparations, and patients in early stages of cancer received "constitutional remedies." He considered diet important.

Eli G. Jones, MD, PhD, graduated from the

Eclectic Medical College and Dartmouth Medical College. He successfully treated his first cancer patient for a blood disease in 1869. He said he cured 80% of his patients by treating cancer as a local manifestation of a constitutional disease. He claimed that he achieved 95% cures for patients who arrived prior to receiving any other cancer therapy.

Survival rates for surgically treated cancer patients in Jones' time were poor. Dr. LeRoy d'Etoilles reported to the French National Academy of Sciences in 1884 what was probably the first 5 year cancer survival study. It was called *The Utility of Surgical Operations in Cancer*. It covered the experience of 174 practitioners and 2,781 patients diagnosed with cancer in 1873. The treatment offered was surgery and caustics such as nitric acid, sulphuric acid, compounds of lead, mercury, or arsenic, zinc sulphate, calcium oxide and potassium permanganate. These were standard treatments until the availability of radium in 1903. The report said that about 67% of the patients survived including 1,172 patients who refused treatment. Only about 42% of those treated with the conventional methods of that time survived for five years.

Jones stated: "To cut out a cancer is the worst form of malpractice for it is only trying to remove the effect without touching the cause. After surgery, cancer returns, often in less than a year, more virulent than before surgery, partly because of the trauma of surgery." He thought that the search for cytotoxic drugs was misguided. He also called those who depended solely on escharotics quacks because, in his opinion, cancer was a constitutional condition affecting the blood and must be treated internally as well as externally. Cures depended first on the vitality of the patient and second the response of his system to remedies.

Jones treated digestion first to restore vitality and to reduce worry. He used strychnine sulfate to restore the nervous system and counteract the effects of radiation. He was the first physician to use poke root (phytolacca) in cancer treatments and believed that fibroid tumors were best treated with that agent. He also recommended Epsom salt baths.

Physicians with cancer came to Jones for treatment. In 40 years of practice, he treated 20,000 cancer patients including 4,300 cases of breast cancer. One involved a 4½ pound breast tumor 22 inches in circumference. He said he relied heavily on the British Dr. Burnett's book describing 132 homeopathic breast cancer cures. He claimed that once cured, his patients stayed cured.

In 1894, Jones started giving seminars, and in 1905 and 1911 he published detailed accounts of his protocols for different types of cancer. The centerpiece of his therapy was a syrup called scrofularia compound which included figwort. He also published four escharotics formulas, a yellow healing salve, and various poultices. He wrote books and articles and taught other physicians how to make and use his herbal medications. Unfortunately, his technology was lost in the drive to install scientific medicine in America in the early 1900s.

Some of his observations are interesting. In all countries where insanity is increasing, cancer is a close second. In Chicago, where insanity was increasing faster than anywhere else in the world, cancer increased 812% between 1861 an 1911. Where meat consumption is low, there are fewer cancer cases. At the Grande

Trappe monastery, where diets exclude tea, coffee and meat, reports indicated that there had been no cancer for 27 years.

Frederic Mohs, MD, used escharotics treatment on a large scale. His methods were standard for treatment of basal cell carcinomas in 1999. His book contains instructions for preparing therapeutic pastes.

In recent times, some people have had notable success in dealing with cancer and have provided convincing evidence supporting Bechamp's theory: Royal R. Rife and Virginia Livingston, MD, in this country and Gaston Naessens in France, and now Canada. Naessen's and Rife's stories can be found in Christopher Bird's The Persecution and Trial of Gaston Naessens and Daniel Haley's Politics in Healing.

Naessen, though unaware of the work of Bechamp and Rife, added something new with the identification of a 3-stage cycle involving the somatid (tiny body) in the blood of healthy people and a 16 stage cycle in the blood of sick people. Knowledge of the 16-stage cycle is said to permit the determination, by examination of a blood sample, of whether a patient is precancerous or, alternatively, how far the disease has progressed when cancer is present. He has taught a number of physicians how to use a condenser and adaptor of his design, with conventional microscopes, to see the elements of the 16-stage cycle in their practice. Unfortunately, medical establishments in France, Canada, and the United States do not accept his discoveries and actively oppose utilization of them.

It will be a tragedy of the first magnitude if medical establishments are permitted to destroy Gaston Naessens advancements in medical science the way they destroyed Royal Raymond Rife's. Naessen's discovery of the somatid and its cycles and his applications of this knowledge to degenerative diseases, immunology, organ transplantation, and chemical surgery, need to be disseminated for the benefit of humanity. His microscope technology and his technique, if widely available, might well result in more revolutionary discoveries.

HARRY HOXSEY'S HERBS

Harry Hoxsey's career provides a prime example of a misuse of power by the medical establishment. In the 1920's, he inherited herbal formulas, developed by his grandfather, which had successfully cured cancer patients for many years. Soon after his father's death he was approached by desperate cancer patients who used his humanitarian instincts to overcome his unwillingness to treat anyone before he became a licensed MD. His successes caught the attention of the AMA in 1924. Soon, Dr. Malcolm Harris, who subsequently became president of the AMA in 1929, tried to get Hoxsey to sell his formulas for a pittance. When he refused to sell, particularly because Harris refused to agree that poor people should receive free treatment, the AMA declared war. Subsequently, Hoxsey was subjected to one "dirty trick" after another. For example, they blacklisted him, which prevented him from going to medical school, and forced him to hire physicians to supervise his clinics. Then, after 20 years of curing cancer in Texas (free for indigent patients and about $400 for those able to pay), they prevailed upon the Texas legislature to pass a law making it illegal for physicians to work for non-physicians. Now, patients in the US, Europe, and

Australia have to travel to Mexico to obtain this therapy. The history of Hoxey's experience is summarized in 35 pages of Daniel Haley's book, <u>Politics in Healing</u>.

Patricia Spain Ward of the Congressional office of Technology Assessment investigated the therapeutic effect of the herbs used in Harry Hoxsey's elixir. She found that orthodox scientific research had identified anti-tumor activity for most of the plants used in Hoxsey's internal tonic, but that not all were deemed capable of inhibiting malignancy. Neither the synergy of the mixture or possible immune boosting effect of the herbs has been studied. His paste has been found to be effective for cancer treatment by scores of investigators for well over 80 years.

<u>DR. WILLIAM FREDERICK KOCH'S CARBONYL COMPOUNDS</u>

The suppression of effective new therapies appears to be a specialty of the AMA, and the FDA has actively supported this activity. The case of Dr. William Frederick Koch, MD, PhD, a brilliant medical scientist who discovered an almost miraculously effective new therapy applicable to a wide variety of diseases, is a good example of how they work together.

After receiving his PhD in biochemistry from the University of Michigan in 1916, and his MD from the Detroit College of Medicine in 1918, he resigned a professorship in physiology and began practicing medicine. His reputation as a brilliant research scientist had been established by papers, published in the Journal of Biological Chemistry in 1912 and 1913 before he had earned his PhD. These papers showed that removal of parathyroid glands endangered the lives of patients and caused that procedure to be discontinued. This achievement was noted in a 1913 editorial in the Journal of the AMA (*JAMA*). His parathyroid research led him to hypothesize that disease results from malfunctions of the body's oxidation system, and that carbonyl compounds might be catalysts capable of reactivating the oxidation process. These compounds have highly active structures with the form O=C=C=O.

Koch found such compounds in heart and brain tissues. He also found that when toxins interfered with or destroyed these compounds, disease resulted. He reasoned that if he could replace the carbonyls in sick people, they might recover. Just incidentally, Dr. Otto Warburg won a Nobel Prize in the 1930's by proving that cancer resulted from inadequate oxygenation of cells. Dr. Szent Gyorgyi, another Nobel laureate, stated in a 1974 article that carbonyls control proliferation and, if lacking in cells, cancer results. He noted that Dr. Koch had preceded him in coming to this conclusion.

Koch was given a chance to test his hypothesis in November of 1917. A physician in St. Mary's Hospital in Detroit referred a patient dying of metastatic liver cancer and expected to live no longer than a week for him to autopsy. This referral gave him an opportunity to test his experimental treatment and observe the results. Koch injected a carbonyl-rich extract of heart and brain tissue into the patient. When he came back to the hospital the next week to autopsy the patient, she was nowhere to be found. He thought there had been a mix-up and someone else had done the autopsy. He was astounded in June to have the patient throw her arms around him and thank him for saving her life. She had been told that Koch had left to join the Army. Hospital personnel neglected to tell him that she had been discharged. His experimental treatment had worked on the first try!

In July 1919, he reported his success with the new treatment in the Detroit Medical Journal. Shortly after his publication appeared, Dr. Henry Carstens, representing the editor of *JAMA* pressured him to turn over to the AMA the results of his research, including the information on production of his carbonyl compounds. Dr. Carstens refused, however, to consider an arrangement whereby indigent patients would receive free treatment, and ultimately Koch refused the AMA's offer to make him famous. Koch, who had been praised by the AMA in 1913, was denounced as a quack in 1919 by Dr. Simmons, the editor of *JAMA*. Soon his scientific papers were no longer accepted for publication by US medical journals. An October 1920 article in the New York Medical Record was the last one to appear. His requests for definitive tests of his therapy were ignored.

The results of Koch's therapy sometimes reached the level of miraculous. It seemed that he was able not only to cure diseases, but to correct extensive damage caused by them. For example, a workman, whose cancer had eaten through the bone on one arm, re-grew the missing bone after receiving Koch's therapy. It appears that his medications helped the human body to not only heal, but to repair itself. The wide applicability of Koch's new therapy was bad for the medical establishment's normal business and it fought back.

After years of achievement in the relief of human suffering, in May of 1941 Koch decided to visit

Brazil for a little vacation. While en route to that country he was pressed into service as ship's doctor, being the only physician aboard. As luck would have it, an important Brazilian diplomat with advanced stomach cancer was felled during the voyage by a serious hemorrhage. He quickly recovered after a shot of Koch's medication.

On arrival in Brazil, the diplomat's amazed Brazilian physician asked Koch to treat other patients, among them several high government officials with supposedly incurable diseases. When many of them happily recovered after receiving his therapy, the Minister of War asked Koch to teach the physicians at a large military hospital how to use his therapy and also to teach some chemists how to prepare his medications. A large number of tuberculosis and leprosy patients were treated as well as a few mental patients. In one case of acute dementia, the patient was discharge as cured five days after an injection. A week later, when he arrived at the hospital, Koch was greeted by an irate man who shook a fist at him and berated him in English. He identified himself as a representative of a pharmaceutical company and said, "We are going to see to it that you don't interfere with our business in South America anymore." A few weeks later, the FDA notified Koch that they wanted to discuss labeling of his products with him personally.

Meanwhile, in mid-March of 1942 in Canada, the governing party decided to invite Koch to Alberta for clinical demonstrations of his therapy. One week after receiving the invitation, late in the evening of Good Friday, Koch was arrested in Del Ray Beach, Florida, and jailed in Miami. At his arraignment, a $10,000 bond was demanded, a very large sum in those days, by the local District Attorney at the request of the FDA, which did not want him to go back to finish his work in Brazil.

This was the first indictment under the federal law, passed in 1938, to prevent the sale of unsafe medicines. The FDA never claimed Koch's products were unsafe. They objected to the label which suggested that they were useful against asthma and cancer. The FDA claimed that they had to be ineffective because the FDA's chemists were unable to distinguish them from distilled water. Consequently, the labeling was false, fraudulent, and deceptive. Actually, these medications were homeopathic dilutions of glycolic and malonic acid anhydrides and found to be such by chemists at the Dow Chemical Co. Later, the FDA claimed that there were no such compounds, and that glycolic and malonic acid were the active ingredients and solutions of these acids, prepared by FDA chemists, had no beneficial effects on diseased mice. The FDA carefully avoided testing Koch's actual products, probably because they feared that they might work. The two involved, and expensive, criminal trials kept him under indictment and prevented him from leaving the country for 4 years.

After years of expensive legal harassment by the FDA and the FTC, Koch got on a plane at Willow Run Airport in Detroit on Thanksgiving Day 1948, and left for Brazil. He said that he could no longer afford to live in his own country. His legal defenses had cost him about $400,000 – equivalent to about $4,000,000 now.

He went back to his research in Brazil and found that his therapy might also be able to cure hoof and mouth disease. In 1955, he was asked to treat polio cases in a ward of the Hospital de Jesus in Rio de

Janeiro. A young girl with polio was kept in another ward until paralyzed and then turned over to Koch, perhaps in an attempt to discredit him. His therapy, however, worked another miracle and a week later she was no longer paralyzed. Soon after this event his reception at the hospital cooled. The Minister of Health found that he was powerless to change the situation and resigned. The hospital administrator, when faced with the choice to either continue Koch's hospital privileges or receive shipments of pharmaceuticals, chose the latter.

In 1964, Koch's health began to fail and in 1967, before he could complete arrangements to take a group of American physicians to Germany and teach them his technology, a stroke deprived him of the power of speech. He died in December of that year. Meanwhile the AMA successfully discouraged use of his therapy among physicians in the US. Orders for his products, manufactured by an organization of protestant ministers, dried up and they discontinued production. In Dan Haley's eloquent words, "The Medical Camelot came to an end."

In a few short years, a simple and remarkably effective new medical technology was born and died. The assassination was conducted by the FDA and the FTC, our Federal Government's designated protectors of our health and pocketbooks, apparently for the benefit of the AMA and the pharmaceutical industry.

ROYAL RAYMOND RIFE'S MICROSCOPES AND RAY MACHINES

In the 1920's and 30's Royal Raymond Rife built

about five super microscopes. One of them, his Universal microscope, was said to be capable of 50,000X magnification with excellent resolution, although experts claimed that 2,000X magnification was the theoretical limit. In addition, his illumination system allowed him to view things with narrow frequency bands that he could vary at will. Details of his microscope were provided in an article published by both the Franklin Institute in Philadelphia and the Smithsonian in Washington, D.C., in l947. The same article described the new RCA electron microscope.

One of Rife's objectives was to determine the cause of cancer. With considerable difficulty, he found a very tiny microbe which could be isolated from cancerous tissue and, when injected into an animal, caused cancer. He called this microbe BX. Very likely it was the same microbe that Virginia Livingston characterized in 1947, progenitor cryptocides. Rife had found that microorganisms could be made to fluoresce at specific frequencies of light for purposes of identification and that they could also be destroyed when exposed to certain frequencies. Rife claimed that he could find a Mortal Oscillatory Rate (MOR) for various pathogenic organisms and directed his research accordingly, culturing and testing various pathogens. Using his Universal #3 microscope, and his directed radio frequency energy 'beam ray' tube machine, Rife claimed to have documented the precise frequencies which destroyed specific organisms. According to the San Diego Evening Tribune in 1938 "We do not wish at this time," Rife commented, "to claim that we cured cancer, or any other disease, for that matter. But we can say that these waves or the 'ray' has the power of devitalizing disease organisms, of 'killing' them, when tuned to an exact particular wave length, or frequency, for each different organism. This applies to the organisms both in their free state and, with certain exceptions, when they are in living tissues."[19]

In 1934, a test on 16 terminal cancer patients demonstrated that this radiation could heal humans. They were exposed to the blue light of a Rife Ray machine for three minutes every third day for 90 days. University of California physicians involved in the test found 15 of them cured. The 16th took another month to heal. In 1937, the Beam Ray company was established to manufacture Rife's machine. A small number of them were built and distributed to interested physicians. Two went to England and about eight to physicians in Southern California. Some physicians used these machines for over 20 years, curing patients of many diseases besides cancer, syphilis, and senile cataracts with this gentle therapy.

In the early 1930's, the editor of *JAMA*, Dr. Morris Fishbein, warned physicians against electronic medicine. In 1939, the San Diego Medical Society warned the physicians who had been using the Rife technology to stop or risk losing their licenses. They also mounted a legal attack on Rife himself. The net result was the end of his research. His research notes, books and papers, microphotographs, and movies illustrating pleomorphism were destroyed in a mysterious fire, and he became an alcoholic. Rife is said to have died in a hospital as the result of being given a drug that had a fatal effect on alcoholics. The official

---

19 '*Processing Infectious Disease Threats*' by the Association of State and Territorial Directors of Health Promotion and Public Health Education. (Internet 8 August 2010).

100

records indicate that he died of a heart attack on August 5, 1971.

In 1954, the Committee on Cancer Diagnosis and Therapy of the National Research Council "evaluated" the Rife Ray Machine. Without inspecting the instrument, testing it, or consulting physicians who had used it, they concluded that it couldn't work. In 1972, the Director of the National Cancer Institute, Dr. Carl G. Baker, used their evaluation to brush off questions about it from the Congressman from San Diego.

In 1960, agents of the government entrapped John Crane and John March, who had taken over manufacture and sale of the Ray Machine and charged them with the illegal practice of medicine. The FDA then made these machines illegal to use and confiscated them - even out of physicians' offices. I understand that they are now also illegal to use in Canada.

DR. VIRGINIA LIVINGSTON WHEELER

In the 1940's, Virginia Wuerthele-Gaspe Livingston, MD, found that bacteria derived from cancerous tissues could cause cancer when injected into animals. In 1969, at a meeting of the New York Academy of Sciences, she reported on research by her group of colleagues which clearly indicated that cancer was caused by an organism which she named Actinomycetales Progenitoracae Cryptocides (which in Latin means "arm-like processes primitive hidden killer.")

At the request of the New York Academy of Science, Livingston set about characterizing the cancer microbe that she had discovered. In 1970, she and Eleanor Jackson, PhD, published a full description of

101

progenitor cryptocides, a tiny microbe found in tumor tissues and body fluids of cancer patients. This microbe could pass through filters designed to separate bacteria from viruses but could be cultivated like a bacterium. In her book Notes on Cancer, she mentions that, in the previous century, Rudolph Virchow may also have seen cryptocides in action. He reported seeing small coccus-like particles dividing inside cancer cells and thought that cancer was caused by parasites.

Like Antoine Bechamp in France and Guenther Enderline in Germany, Livingston claimed that elements of the microbe were present in every human cell, and were responsible for initiating life, and for killing us with cancer and other diseases. She also found, as they had, that this microbe was pleomorphic, it could change shape and size as its environment changed.

In 1973, at a New York American Medical Association Exhibition, press coverage of Livingston's exhibit, which showed cancer microbes on a TV screen, was prevented by Dr. Rhodes, an official of the association. Rhodes also forced Livingston to terminate her research. He persuaded the trustee of a foundation, who was dying of cancer, to give him the right to approve the use of the $750,000 grant which was supposed to fund it.

In 1976, Livingston was granted patent No. 3958025 for the treatment of a vitamin deficiency of abscisic acid in man, animals, and avian species as related to the prevention or suppression of cancer by this vitamin. A state with a large chicken industry, plagued with chicken cancer, is said to have licensed her patent. Abcissic acid is part of vitamin A. Liver enzymes can release it from carrots.

102

As a clinician, Livingston is reported to have treated many cancer patients, including Dr. Owen Wheeler, her future husband. Together they wrote five books on the microbiology of cancer. Shortly before her death, she was ordered by California medical authorities to cease treating cancer patients because her method of treatment was not in accordance with the law, which stipulated exactly how cancer patients were to be treated. Despite the legal harassment, Livingston continued to treat patients until her death at 83.

Soon after her death, in March 1990, an unsigned, highly critical article about the therapy used in the Livingston-Wheeler Clinic appeared in the American Cancer Society sponsored *"CA: Cancer Journal for Physicians."* This article stated that progenitor cryptocides do not exist, that the therapy used in the clinic was faulty, that there was no evidence that a defective immune system could result in cancer, or that a whole foods diet restores immune system deficiencies.

The elimination of Harry Hoxsey's herbs, Dr. Koch's remarkable homeopathic therapy, and Royal Raymond Rife's Ray Machines from the practice of medicine in the US can hardly be said to have benefited the citizens of this country. Has the power to regulate the practice of medicine, granted by the Congress to the AMA, been used for the benefit of the public? These examples of the treatment of medical innovations justify doubt. If these three cancer treatments had been widely available in 1971, no war on cancer could have been justified. Millions of our people would not have experienced the torture of chemotherapy or have had to watch their life savings melt away during the last few years of their lives.

Furthermore, if Virginia Livingston's research

had not been terminated in 1973 by Dr. Rhodes, an AMA official, shortly after the war on cancer began, the war might soon have ended. How he managed to get a dying trustee to change an allocation of funds is unknown. Although Livingston's research was not confirmed, there is a very high probability, almost a certainty, that a microbe causes cancer, Wilhelm Reich's Tod bacteria, and Rife's BX are most likely to have been manifestations of cryptocides. With research on its defeat in the hands of a competent medical scientist with adequate funds, $750,000 in 1970 dollars, the waste of billions of dollars on cancer research could have been avoided in my opinion. A scientifically characterized microbe cannot be obliterated by the stroke of a pen wielded by a medical doctor. It may yet infect the AMA.

CANCER AND VITAMIN C

Investigations of the effect of vitamin C on cancer have a long history. In 1973, Irwin Stone's book, The Healing Factor - Vitamin C Against Disease reported that German research in 1940 and 1956 had indicated that vitamins C and E in large quantities had value in controlling cancer in some cases. Ewan Cameron's book, Hyaluronidas and Cancer in 1966 noted that malignant tumors generated an enzyme that weakened intercellular cement and facilitated invasion by cancer cells. He noted that strengthening this cement could help resist the spread of cancer. In 1971, Linus Pauling suggested that ascorbic acid in large doses should strengthen intercellular cement by increasing synthesis of collagen fibrils. Soon Cameron and Pauling were collaborating and Cameron began treating

104

terminal cancer patients with large doses of ascorbate. He found that this not only extended their lives, but substantially reduced their pain. Patients taking large doses of morphine no longer needed the drug. Vitamin C acted like aspirin to inhibit synthesis of prostaglandins but, unlike aspirin, it increased the synthesis of PEG1 to enhance the immune system. Reduction in malignant activity was also observed. It was time for a controlled trial.

Since Cameron was unwilling to deprive any of his patients of vitamin C, in 1973, Pauling suggested that the National Cancer Institute review Cameron's case histories and support a clinical trial. NCI authorities insisted that animal studies come first and that Pauling should apply for a grant for an animal study at the University of California. Pauling's grant application was approved by the NCI's consultants, but the NCI waited eight years - until 1981 - to provide partial support for this study!

In 1979, Morishgi and Murata published the results of a 5 year study at the Fukuoka Hospital in Japan that confirmed Cameron's findings. On the other hand, Moertel et. al. at the Mayo Clinic performed two controlled trials which, they claimed, refuted the Scottish and Japanese studies. But Moertel et. al. did not replicate the previous studies. They gave patients less than 10 grams for only 2.5 months after which patients received no more vitamin C. Furthermore, the Moertel report suppressed the fact that their patients had been taken off vitamin C, and had not been receiving it for a median of 10.5 months before they died. This is important because stopping this treatment abruptly is known to cause the liver to remove vitamin C from the immune system thus reducing resistance to infection.

Cameron's patients continued to receive it for the rest of their lives – some for 14 years. NCI's Dr. R. E. Wittes also suppressed this information, and joined with Moertel in recommending that no more studies of vitamin C be conducted.

In 1992, Mattius Rath published a paper in the *Journal of Orthomolecular Medicine* which, in essence, said that the essential amino acid L-lysine supplements the action of natural enzyme blockers to stop plasmin and collegenase from breaking down the tissues and ground substance that holds cells in place and maintains the integrity of body structures. He believes that the $100 million international market for chemotherapeutic drugs is the reason why there is so little progress in cancer research.

Presently, Dr. Hunninghake and his fellow physicians at the Riordan Clinic in Wichita, Kansas, formerly the Center for the Improvement of Human Functioning, provide intravenous sodium ascorbate to patients undergoing conventional cancer therapy. However, this treatment is not part of the Standards of Care and is not generally available.

CHELATION REDUCES CANCER RISK

More than 20 years ago, scientists from the Institute for Radiation Therapy and Nuclear Medicine at the University of Zurich discovered that chelation therapy substantially reduced cancer death rates among Swiss citizens exposed to lead from automobile exhausts. Aware of the importance of this discovery and the controversy that might arise because of it, Drs. W. Blumer and T. Reich submitted their data to a skeptical epidemiologist for review. He could find nothing wrong, so they published their findings in a 1980 issue of *Environmental International*.

Their paper disclosed that only 1 of 59 people who had received chelation therapy died of cancer during their 18 years of monitoring the group exposed to high traffic. In comparison, 30 of the 172 people who did not receive chelation – the rest of the 231 people with high traffic exposure – died during the same period. Clearly, chelation therapy had reduced cancer risk by more than 90% in this experiment. Deaths from all causes were also lower among these fortunate Swiss.

Dr. Bruce Halstead, author of <u>The Scientific Basis of Chelation Therapy</u>, suggested that reduction in levels of free radicals resulting from the removal of iron, copper, lead, and other heavy metals from the bloodstream was responsible for the major benefits of this therapy. Dr. H. B. Demopoulos of New York Medical Center found that heavy metals, free radicals, and oxidized fats were associated with the initiation of cancer. Consequently, there is a plausible theoretical basis for the conclusion that chelation therapy can reduce cancer death rates.

<u>LOW DOSE WHOLE BODY X-RAY TREATMENTS</u>

The December 7, 2007, *New York Times* clearly stated a serious problem for patients with non-Hodgkin's lymphoma: Medicare officials are unwilling to pay what suppliers want to charge for some new last-ditch medications. The medications were Bexxar from GlaxoSmithKline, and Zevalin from Biogen Idec. Both drugs contain radioactive materials and require administration by specially licensed technicians and physicians. Both came on the market within the preceding 5 years.

New Medicare rules, which took effect on 1 January, 2008, provide for a $16,000 reimbursement of hospitals per treatment, but the market price for each drug is about $30,000 per treatment. These drugs are expensive, but then a year of chemotherapy can cost $50,000.

The Times noted that each year about 60,000 people discover that they are victims of this disease and about 20,000 die because of it. These new drugs are usually prescribed for patients who have not responded to other therapies. One treatment can put the disease in remission for a few years. A recent test of 414 patients showed that Zevalin and chemotherapy put lymphomas in remission for three years versus one year for chemotherapy alone. The new Medicare rules threaten to prevent thousands of patients from using this therapy, sometimes the only one available to them according to the Lymphoma Research Foundation.

A Deputy Administrator of The Centers for Medicare and Medicaid Services, which oversees Medicare, disclosed that his Agency recognized the value of these drugs, but doesn't want to overpay for them. He claims that hospitals have been paying only $16,000, and that is a fair price. The companies that sell the drugs, and the hospitals that purchase them, apparently disagree.

It would be nice to have less expensive alternatives to $16,000 treatments for this disease. Fortunately, there is one. Early promising results were obtained in 1975, over 30 years ago, at the Harvard Medical School, when physicians treated lymphoma patients with low dose whole body radiation. These results were confirmed in 1977, also at Harvard, and later by Dr. Sakamoto in Japan. His lymphoma patients received 150 rads of X rays in 10 or 15 whole body treatments. Thirteen years later 84% of them were still alive. He was so convinced of the value of low dose whole body radiation that, after surgery for metastasized colon cancer, he gave himself two treatments and is now reported to be free of the disease. His experience indicates that it might be broadly useful against many varieties of cancer.

The FDA has approved treatment of minor cases of lymphoma with low dose whole body radiation; although test results on which approval was based included major cases. This therapy is not much used because, according to an authority at the National Institutes of Health, "it is too easy." Perhaps it is also too inexpensive!

FUTURE MEDICAL RESEARCH

Not everyone is capable of making new scientific discoveries. They are not the automatic result of investments in facilities and manpower. Nor are they facilitated by government control of distribution of research funds. This is particularly true in areas where political interests are involved. It is too easy to foster politically modified science which all too often results in misinformation and waste.

While Rife and Livingston-Wheeler are dead, Gaston Naessens, in his 70's, was very much alive when I visited his laboratory in Rock Forest, Quebec, a few years ago. Another genius, he also designed and built an unusual microscope capable of 30,000 times magnification. A rarity in modern times, he was able to conduct independent research because of support from his affluent family and friends. It would be a great loss to have his unique fund of medical knowledge remain unexploited by a medical system committed to obsolete technologies. His know-how could revolutionize practice in several fields of medicine including transplant surgery, in my opinion.

CHAPTER 5 - INFECTIOUS DISEASES

160,000 Americans die every year of infectious diseases, a far cry from the 500,000 a year who die of cancer, but HIV/AIDS and pneumonia/influenza are listed among the 10 leading causes of death. These diseases are human illnesses caused by viruses, bacteria, parasites, fungi, and other microbes. They may be spread by direct contact with an infected person or animal, by ingesting contaminated food or water, by insects like mosquitoes or ticks (disease vectors), or by contact with contaminated surroundings like animal droppings or even contaminated air. In 1996, infectious diseases were reported to have killed one-third of the more than 52 million people who died in that year. They are the leading cause of death worldwide and new diseases continue to appear. According to the World Health Organization, at least 30 have been discovered in the last 20 years.

The total cost of treatment and lost productivity for these diseases exceeds $120 billion a year. They are responsible for 25% of visits to physicians and anti-microbial agents are the second most frequently prescribed drugs.

PNEUMONIA / INFLUENZA

550,000 Americans are reported to have died of influenza during the Spanish Flu (H1N1) epidemic of

1918-1919. The 1956 edition of *Statistical Abstracts of the United States* indicate that deaths from influenza and pneumonia totaled about 430,000 in 1920. Subsequently, death rates per 100,000 decreased from 207 in 1920 to 103 in 1930, 70.3 in 1940 and reached 27.5 in 1955. There is no separate listing for deaths from influenza, possibly because the disease frequently converts into pneumonia and patients die from that instead of the flu. The 1996 edition of the *Abstract* lists them separately. In 1970, 59,000 Americans died of pneumonia and only 3,700 died of influenza; and in 1993, 80,700 died of pneumonia but only 1,100 died of influenza. The rates per 100,000 in 1993 were 31.3 for pneumonia and 0.4 for influenza. The above information indicates that either the influenza viruses had lost most of their virulence by 1940, or that treatments for the disease were less lethal, or both.

In 1944, Drs. Salk and Francis, under an Army contract at the University of Michigan's School of Public Health perfected the first inactivated flu vaccine widely used by the US forces during World War II. Since then, each year the CDC guesses what strains of the flu are likely to be common in the next flu season and then develops and promotes a vaccine for those strains.

Currently, there are eight different flu vaccines, three of which do not contain thimerosol [20] and three

---

20 Thimerosal is a mercury-containing organic compound (an organomercurial). Since the 1930s, it has been widely used as a preservative in a number of biological and drug products, including

others are available with reduced thimerosol formulations.

Recent research, published in the November 1, 2009, issue of *Clinical Infectious Diseases*, indicates that misuse of aspirin may have been partially responsible for the high death rates during the flu pandemic. High doses of aspirin are known to cause toxicity and can lead to a dangerous build-up of fluid in the lungs. Autopsy reports from 1918 are consistent with what we now know about aspirin toxicity, according to Karen Starko, the author of the article. She suggested that physicians at that time did not understand either the dosing or pharmacology of aspirin but were willing to recommend its use because it was promoted by drug companies and endorsed by physicians anxious to "do something." Desperate families and institutions accepted it in the hope that it would benefit their loved ones.

Unfortunately, the death rate for hospitalized patients treated by regular allopathic physicians was about 30%, probably due, in part, to the results of aspirin toxicity. This compares with a 1.07% death rate for the 62,000 hospitalized patients of homeopathic physicians who used benign homeopathic medications and a 0.7% death rate for their patients who didn't need hospitalization.

---

many vaccines, to help prevent potentially life threatening contamination with harmful microbes.

Evidently, homeopathic physicians, who spent a lot of time studying all of the symptoms of their patients and prescribing small amounts of a remedy which could produce the same symptoms in a well person, experienced low death rates. Unfortunately, there were not many of them: and the AMA was discrediting homeopaths and forcing their schools to close during this period.

On the other hand, physicians educated in AMA controlled schools, which provided little training in pharmacology and made them dependent on drug companies for information about remedies, wound up killing some of their patients with over doses of aspirin. The drug companies were selling aspirin's advantages as treatment for symptoms like fever, headaches, and pain, symptoms of influenza. Inadequately trained physicians, anxious to cure their influenza patients, urged on by an uninformed public to do something, prescribed lots of aspirin, converting their influenza into pneumonia, which killed many of the patients.

Dr. Fredrick Klenner, as a child, lived on a farm in Pennsylvania during the flu pandemic. He stated that his family was not affected by the flu, although many people in their area died from it. He believed that his family's habit of taking a heavy dose of an herbal infusion, which he later found contained vitamin C, at the first sign of a cold or the flu, protected them from infection. In his practice in later years, he used multi-gram injections of sodium ascorbate to cure all kinds of viral diseases, including the flu and polio.

AIDS

According to the CDC more than one million Americans had AIDS in 2009 and about 21% are unaware of their infection. About 56,000 Americans are infected, and 18,000 are killed, by the AIDS virus every year.

In the past decade, anti-retroviral therapies have been developed which, in combination, reduce the replication rate of the HIV virus which is said to cause the disease. This has led to increased life expectancies for AIDS patients, but according to the CDC, there is no known cure for the disease at this time.

In 1995, the *Los Angeles Times* reported that by 2000 the total cost of the AIDS pandemic could reach $514 billion. In 2002, the estimated annual cost of caring for an individual with advanced AIDS was $34,000 according to the Kaiser Family Foundation which based its estimate on a study by Michael Saag at the University of Alabama.

In view of the high prices for antiviral drugs, the South African Government passed a law making their production in South Africa legal despite the fact that they were still protected by patents. As a result, 39 drug companies sued the South African Government in the late 1990's. In 2001, facing vast international humanitarian pressures, they gave up. Cipla, an Indian company, promptly drove the international price of antiretroviral drug therapy from over $10,000 annually to as little as $300 annually with generic copies of the three drugs, stavudine, amivudine and nevirapine, currently used to treat AIDS patients.

The syndrome AIDS, which started out as an infection associated with homosexual males and intravenous drug users, is now widespread—a worldwide scourge. Robert Gallo of the National Cancer Institute, Lac Montagnier of the Pasteur Institute, and Dr. Jay Levy of the University of California have all reported isolation of a virus responsible for this disease. According to theory the human immunodeficiency virus, two thin strands of ribonucleic acid (RNA) wrapped in a protein coat, destroys T4 cells, important elements of the immune system. Without an effective immune system the AIDS patient is vulnerable to all sorts of diseases and ultimately dies because of this vulnerability.

Dr. Peter Duesberg, a retro virologist and member of the Department of Biology of the University of California at Berkeley, named California scientist of the year in 1971, noted that the S in AIDS stands for "syndrome," which means that it is not a single disease entity. In the March 1989 issue of the magazine *Cancer Research*, he also noted that even in dying AIDS patients it is very difficult to detect this virus and antigens to it. He also noted that many members of the AIDS research establishment have a financial interest in testing kits, and the companies that make and sell them, which can affect their objectivity.

There is reason to suspect that this very complex disease called AIDS may possibly be caused by a

116

pleomorphic microbe. If so, it may be curable by therapies based on the research of Antoine Bechamp and Gunther Enderline. Isopathic therapies use homeopathic doses of biological preparations.

ISOPATHIC THERAPY

Two hundred years of research on pleomorphic microorganism has been disregarded by conventional medicine for too long. It is a fact that isopathic therapies, based on this research, have been successfully used to cure disease for over 50 years. And these therapies have helped AIDS patients.

The human body is not sterile. Even sperm cells contain tiny microbes that have useful functions. Virginia Livingston, MD, found that progenitor cryptocides, which she characterized with Eleanor Jackson, PhD, was able to produce choriogonadotropin, a cell growth regulator which, she claimed, protected fertilized eggs from destruction as a foreign body. This primitive organism lives with us throughout our lives in a symbiotic relationship when our bodies are healthy, but it can change shape, size, and function when poor diet, stress, and toxins change the internal conditions of the body. It can turn into virulent, pathogenic forms associated with diseases. Isopathic therapies can be used to treat such diseases.

Isopathy is defined as 'the treatment of disease by use of the causal agent or a product of the same disease or treatment of a diseased organ with an extract of a similar healthy organ.' Isopathic remedies are approved by the FDA for use in the United States, are manufactured in Germany by SANUM, and are obtainable from Pleomorphic Sanum Co. in Glendale, Arizona. Their internet address is PleoSANUM.com.

Swiss biologist Dr. Bruno Haefli uses isopathic therapies. He believes that growth forms of fungi may be involved in AIDS. Juliane Sacher, MD, working in the 1980's, stated that 85% of her AIDS patients remained stable or improved after 18 months of treatment with the holistic treatments, and SANUM products Pefrakehl and Notakehl, plus ozone. In Sweden, Dr. Erik Enby also reported success in treating AIDS patients with Utilin and Nigersan. He found that patients improved dramatically and their blood picture under the microscope became healthier. He believes that the AIDS-causing microbe is pleomorphic and causes different diseases as it develops through different stages. Like many physicians whose research efforts lead them off the proscribed path of scientific medicine, Dr. Enby's license was revoked in 2007.

Dr. Karl Andreas Guischard used SANUM biological medications and ozone therapy and found that he could halt the progress of the syndrome. His attempts to interest professors at the University of Hamburg in undertaking clinical studies were rebuffed, however. When he presented his results on 25 patients showing how blood factors normalized after 50 days, he was asked if he was sure the syndrome was AIDS. His results were declared unbelievable.

LET'S TRY ISOPATHIC THERAPY AGAINST TUBERCULOSIS

There is a large reservoir of multi drug resistant tuberculosis (MDRTB) in India where 30% of the world's TB patients are located. About 2 million Indians acquire the disease every year and someone dies because of it every minute. With easy movement of people around the world, the potential for spreading of the TB infection is obvious. About 1,266 million legal immigrants entered our country in 2006 including 5,872 from India. Indians are among the fastest growing ethnic groups in the country. There were 1.68 million of them here in 2000 and 2.57 million in 2007. Our immigration laws were designed to provide protection against importation of disease, but health provisions are no longer adequately enforced.

Tuberculosis was our second leading cause of death for the first half of last century. The bacilli causing it were defeated by antibiotics, but they are becoming antibiotic resistant. It could, once again, become a major killer of Americans. In 2000, about 16,000 American had TB and between 10 and 15 million of us carried a latent TB infection. About 10% of latent infections are expected to develop into the disease. It would seem to be an ideal candidate for a trial of Isopathic Therapy since a very effective Isopathic cure for this disease was developed 100 years ago.

In 1903, Prof. Friedrich Franz Friedman, MD, a young Jewish physician in Germany, developed a biological medication for the treatment of tuberculosis, which reduced and sometimes eliminated the need for costly operations or long cures in sanitaria. Operators of German sanitaria were not pleased and criticized his treatment, vociferously. It was also a threat to the chemotherapy industry. Nevertheless, by 1912, successful treatment of nearly 15,000 patients established its efficacy. In 1914, Paul Ehrlich, a Nobel laureate, was put in charge of a commission to evaluate Friedman's discovery. In 1922, the Prussian National Assembly commission declared his medication harmless and surprisingly effective, if used early, against all forms of tuberculosis.

Enderlein studied the effects of Friedman's medication and found that one or two injections of it halved tuberculosis infestations in the lungs. The effect continued to destroy the disease until, in many cases, it completely disappeared.

Friedman is reported to have lectured before the US Congress about his discovery. Subsequently, the US Government Printing Office is said to have published a 54-page document titled <u>Dr. Friedman's New Treatment for Tuberculosis</u>. President Teddy Roosevelt is reported to have sent him a letter of appreciation wishing him success in his work.

Unfortunately, an attempt to introduce Friedman's methods into the United States ran into a brick wall in Saranac Lake, N.Y., where the Trudeau

Sanitarium for Treatment of Tuberculosis, and a thriving "cure cottage" industry was well established. According to Alfred Donaldson's History of the Adirondacks, Friedman sold the bottling rights of his cure to an American syndicate that leased the Algonquin Hotel on Lower Saranac Lake for use as a sanitarium for the Friedman treatment of tuberculosis in the spring of 1913. The venture proved to be ill advised and ephemeral. On May 29th, 1913, the New York City Board of Health unanimously passed a new regulation aimed directly at the Friedman treatment, effectively prohibiting its continued use. The company closed its doors on Jan. 21, 1914.

Almost 100 years later, the technology of the information age may allow American TB patients another chance to learn and experience the surprisingly effective therapy pioneered by Friedrich Franz Friedman, MD.

BACTERIAL DISEASES

In 2007, reports indicate that Americans used over 50 million pounds of antibiotics. About 70% of that total was used in food production and, as a result, they are showing up in water supplies. Antibiotics have saved a lot of lives - and killed a lot of bacteria. They are still regular prescription items for physicians, but 65 years of intensive use have had unfortunate consequences. Bacteria have become resistant and are taking their revenge. Untreatable bacterial infections are killing about 100,000 of us every year according to Professor Robert L. Dorit at Smith College whose article in a recent <u>American Scientist</u> presents an overview of antibiotics.

Between 1943 and 1945 extensive use on battlefields caused the production of about 100 million doses of penicillin, the first of the antibiotics. Before the end of the war some bacteria were already penicillin-resistant. Since then, many new antibiotics have been developed, but each time the pattern repeats; the bacteria adapt. The time between introduction of a new antibiotic and the appearance of resistant bacteria is three to five years.

Natural selection encourages survivors to adapt, and bacteria have evolved, producing packages of resistance elements. Some of these include multiple genes encoding resistance to as many as 74 different antibiotics. Under antibiotic threat, bacteria are able to obtain resistance elements from the environment and from other bacteria as well.

Research at McMasters University revealed that soil bacteria contain rudimentary resistance to all known antibiotics - even synthetic ones with no natural equivalent. Researchers at Harvard Medical School have recently found that hundreds of different soil bacteria can actually subsist on antibiotics. In other words, they can use them as food!

The wonder drugs of the last half of the 20th century are losing their luster. More and more bacteria are adjusting to their threat. Mainstream medicine has inadvertently created new varieties that are very difficult and sometimes impossible to defeat. The prolific indiscriminate use of antibiotics is causing serious problems. Alternatives to antibiotics which will not lead to a whole new breed of super bacteria would appear to be desirable. Fortunately there are some. Isopathic Therapies, colloidal silver and chlorine dioxide offer considerable promise.

VIRAL DISEASES

Many diseases are caused by viruses for which there are few effective drugs, but here nature has provided a remedy, a panacea for a wide variety of infectious diseases, which plays an essential role in our immune systems. This is vitamin C, in the form of ascorbic acid or sodium ascorbate, an inexpensive substance which has remained unrecognized and underutilized by our medical establishment for over 50 years. Its effectiveness is enhanced by vitamin D-3, the sunshine vitamin, now considered to be a hormone. Vitamin D-3 has very recently been found to be an important factor in immune system activities. Nevertheless, some medical authorities still discourage patients from taking more than the amount of vitamin C needed to prevent scurvy, and more vitamin D-3 than that required to prevent rickets.

Hippocrates (460-370 BC) described scurvy, a terminal illness, in which healed wounds reopen, teeth were lost and the internal organs, on autopsy, appeared similar to those of cancer patients. He probably observed a multiple-deficiency variant of the disease because modern experiments produce slightly different symptoms. Scurvy involves general inhibition of metabolic reactions for which vitamin C is a co-factor. When a body's supply of vitamin C is exhausted, fibroblasts are unable to produce collagen, osteoblasts do not synthesize osteoid, and odontoblasts don't synthesize dentine. In other words, maintenance and repair systems cease functioning and the body starts to fall apart. The underlying defect is lack of conversion of the internally produced amino acid proline to hydroxyproline.

Years ago scurvy used to ravage the crews of naval vessels on long voyages. The British found a solution to maritime scurvy in the form of a ration of citrus fruits - hence the word "Limey" to describe British sailors. The determination of how much was enough citrus fruit to prevent scurvy among the young men of ships' crews probably led to the idea of "minimum daily requirements." Unfortunately, this focus on preventing scurvy in healthy young men may have caused health authorities to overlook the fact that we are not all healthy young men. The predilection of powerful bureaucracies to stick to a decision once made, has given rise to the myth that all the ascorbic acid anyone needs is what is sufficient to prevent scurvy in healthy young men. This myth still distorts the thinking of many medical school faculties, their students, and practicing physicians.

Vitamin C is required for the production of collagen, which holds our bodies together, for the hydroxylation of tryptophan to 5 hydroxy tryptopfan, which has a profound effect on the peripheral vascular system and it also acts like aspirin to reduce pain without aspirins adverse effects on the immune system.

SZENT GYORGYI ON MEDICAL USE OF VITAMIN C

Vitamin C was first isolated in 1928, and synthesized in 1933. Albert Szent-Gyorgyi, MD, a Hungarian, received a Nobel Prize for its discovery in 1938. A considerable amount of research on the vitamin was reviewed by Stewart C. P. Lind in the Bicentennial Symposium at Edinborough in 1953 and by S. W. H. Schieb and H. R. S. Harris in *The Vitamins: Chemistry, Physiology and Pathology*, Vol. 1 N.Y., Academic Press. From then until 1973, little additional research was undertaken and there was an insufficiency of understanding about its cellular biochemistry.

Szent-Gyorgyi has been quoted as saying, "I always had the feeling that not enough use was made of it, vitamin C, for supporting human health," and "the medical profession took a very narrow and wrong view." He noted that scurvy is not the first symptom of lack of this vitamin, but a pre-mortal syndrome. It is not sensible to recommend that people limit their intake of vitamin C to just enough to prevent death by scurvy. They need enough to support full health. He observed that, unfortunately, nobody knows what full health is, although it could be found by statistical studies. Linus Pauling said that the amount of vitamin C required for full health varies from person to person.

Szent-Gyorgyi stated that if you get a cold because of an insufficiency of vitamin C, which develops into pneumonia, your diagnosis will be pneumonia and not lack of vitamin C.

Other scientists like Irwin Stone, a biochemist, and Linus Pauling, a Nobel Laureate, recognized the great importance of vitamin C in keeping people healthy. They were not alone. Students at MIT were using it to defeat colds and flu in 1939. Unfortunately, while scientists worked hard to convince people of the importance of this vitamin and the need for adequate amounts of it, they were actively opposed by the medical monopoly. The well-organized propaganda mills of organized medicine, backed by propaganda from their allies in the FDA, confused the public and reduced a serious threat to drug company profits. The establishment was assisted by the National Technical Writers Association which had agreed with the AMA that their members didn't understand medicine and science and would seek the approval of medical and scientific authorities before publicizing any stories about new discoveries.

Nevertheless, some far-seeing physicians recognized an opportunity. Their experiments produced important advances in medical science and technology which, if implemented, today could quickly produce substantially lower costs of medical care. The monumental achievements of Fredrick Klenner lie fallow in medical publications, awaiting a renaissance in which physicians become free to use technologies outside the confines of the <u>Standards of Care</u>, and the limitations of the AMA's copyrighted codes which insurance companies use to control the practice of medicine by refusing to pay for medical services inconsistent with their policies.

DR. FREDERICK KLENNER AND VITAMIN C

Frederick Klenner, BS, MS, MD, earned scientific credentials with two degrees in biochemistry before entering medical school. His monumental advancements in medical science have been studiously ignored by medical authorities for over 60 years. If the medical Luddites who block substantial changes in the practice of medicine can be neutralized, his technology could be quickly utilized and yield immediate returns in the form of substantially lower costs of medical care and far healthier Americans, both children and adults.

Klenner called minimum daily requirements for vitamin C an "illegitimate child" "co-fathered by the National Academy of Science and the National Research Council." He called the idea a tragic error in judgment. It might also be called a colossal blunder because there are clear indications that vitamin C deficiency has been responsible for an enormous amount of pain, suffering, disease, death, and medical expense.

His article in the *Journal of Nutrition*, #3 & #4, Winter, 1971, gives substance to this opinion. In it he notes that the demands of our bodies for vitamin C go far beyond the scorbutic (sufficient to prevent scurvy) levels. In support, he quotes from the Department of Agriculture's 1939 Yearbook: "In fact, even when there is not a single outward symptom of trouble, a person may be in a state of vitamin C deficiency more dangerous than scurvy itself. When such a condition is not detected, and continues uncorrected, the teeth and bones will be damaged, and what may be even more serious, the blood stream is weakened to the point where it can no longer resist or fight infections not so easily cured as scurvy."

Klenner's list of factors affecting ascorbic acid needs include:

1. Age of the individual
2. Habits – such as smoking, alcohol use, playing habits
3. Sleep, especially artificially induced sleep
4. Trauma
5. Kidney threshold
6. Environment
7. Physiological stress
8. Season of the year
9. Loss in the stool
10. Variation in individual absorption
11. Variation of binders in vitamin C tablets
12. Body chemistry

13.   Drugs
14.   Pesticides
15.   Body weight
16.   Inadequate storage

Klenner used the vitamin C output of stressed and unstressed rats, converted to the equivalent needs of a 70-kilogram (150 pound) man to provide a basis for treatment of his obstetrical patients. He prescribed 4 to 15 grams of ascorbic acid per day during gestation depending on need. During the last trimester, 20% of his patients took 15 grams per day. A booster injection of 10 grams (as sodium ascorbate) was given to 80% of them on entering the hospital for delivery. The booster injections before delivery helped take care of the stress and pain encountered during that process and speeded up healing after the ordeal.

The results were very beneficial: women who had previously aborted multiple times, did not abort; hemoglobin levels were easier to maintain; leg cramps affected less than 3% and were always associated with running out of vitamin C tablets; labor was of shorter duration and less painful; no postpartum hemorrhages were encountered; no patient required catheterization; infants produced were all robust – none required resuscitation; there were no feeding problems. In fact, the "Fultz Quadruplets", the only ones that had survived in the southeastern United States in his day, were included in his series of 300 cases. Nurses noted that babies in this series were distinctly different and called them Vitamin C Babies!

Although Klenner does not explain why these mothers needed so much ascorbic acid, the reason is now obvious. The growing fetus needs large amounts to produce collagen. This substance is a major component of the matrices that hold body cells in place. It is also a major component of bone, a complex of semiconductors containing collagen and apatite, a calcium phosphate mineral. If mothers are not provided with enough vitamin C to satisfy the needs of their fetuses, they and their babies can suffer unpleasant consequences.

Klenner found that massive doses of sodium ascorbate had positive effects on a wide variety of disease conditions. "The types of pathology treatable with massive doses of ascorbic acid run the entire gamut of medical knowledge." This should not be surprising. Ascorbic acid has long been shown to provide the first line of defense in our immune systems. Since we do not manufacture it internally, the limited amount readily available (about 5 grams in the well nourished) is rapidly used up when disease strikes. As our immune cells run out of the ammunition that they need to continue defending us, our bodies begin to experience the symptoms of disease. It is understandable, therefore, that injecting grams of the sodium salt form of vitamin C into the bloodstream quickly reenergizes our defenses and tilts the odds in favor of our immune system and against attacking pathogens.

What is surprising is the speed and power with which the immune system acts. For example, Klenner injected twelve grams of ascorbate into a man who was in shock, turning blue, and believed he was dying as a result of puss caterpillar bites. By the time the injection was completed his fear and pain had disappeared. Klenner also quickly eliminated a little girl's pain and trauma from the bite of a venomous snake with vitamin C injections. Unfortunately, this treatment is not readily available. When I asked for an infusion of ascorbate to counter a possible brown recluse spider bite, the emergency room physician said that she would provide it after she read about the procedure in the Journal of the American Medical Association. Evidently she didn't want to risk losing her license, or hospital privileges, and/or possibly tangling with a hungry lawyer by functioning outside the limits of the *Standards of Care*. One of my medical friends admitted to curing a case of herpes with vitamin C infusions by accepting the risk of loss of license to practice medicine.

During the polio epidemic in the 1940's, Klenner pioneered an important application of vitamin C. He injected 6 to 20 grams of sodium ascorbate into a series of 60 polio patients. Their polio disappeared within 72 hours. He reported this verbally at the June 10, 1949 meeting of the American Medical Association and subsequently published his experience in detail in the *Southern Surgeon* in July 1949. Although his comments were noted in an article reviewing the meeting by Galloway and Seifert in the Journal of the American

Medical Association during the polio epidemic, this remarkable performance was ignored by the medical establishment: except that one of the vaccine developers is reported to have unsuccessfully tried vitamin C on a monkey infected with polio. Undoubtedly, Klenner's achievement was classed as anecdotal because it had not been confirmed by double blind studies. Meanwhile, thousands of men women and children, afflicted with the disease, either died, lived out their lives in "iron lungs," or became permanently crippled. President Franklin D. Roosevelt was a well known victim.

The 21st Edition of the <u>Cecil Textbook of Medicine</u>, dated 2000, states that "no specific treatment is available" for polio. According to this authoritative work, Klenner's cure of polio with vitamin C injections never happened! People can develop the disease as a result of "protective" injections of polio vaccine, but this remains the only approved method of defeating the virus.

The *Journal of Applied Nutrition,* 1971 – 23: 61-88 contains an article by Klenner proposing the use of high-dose intravenous sodium ascorbate as a treatment for cancer. He reported no ill effects from 150 grams of it ingested during 24 hours. As noted in the chapter on cancer, Linus Pauling and Ewan Cameron also found it useful in alleviating the symptoms of terminal cancer patients. The Riordan Clinic in Wichita, Kansas provides supplemental infusions of vitamin C to cancer patients being treated by conventional oncologists, but such treatments are not widely available, perhaps because they would reduce the sales of narcotic drugs.

Klenner's research indicated that infants with mild colds which lasted for several weeks, or a flu which lasted 48 to 96 hours, complicated by extreme distress, could suddenly exhibit symptoms of encephalitis, and die in 30 minutes to 2 hours of asphyxia. He reported this in an article in the *Tri-State Medical Journal* in 1957. This has all the earmarks of Sudden Infant Death Syndrome (SIDS). His patients survived this emergency situation via immediate massive ascorbate therapy.

It is interesting to note an administrative judge's ruling on SIDS in an FDA action in California:

"Respondent represents that vitamin C deficiency is the cause of SIDS and ingestion of vitamin C by infants will prevent it - This representation is false in fact. Based on the testimony of Drs. Sampson and Wilson, I find that vitamin C is not a positive factor in crib death and that ingestion of ample amounts of vitamin C will not prevent its occurrence. This view conforms to the consensus of informed medical and scientific opinion." Evidently, a consensus of misinformed medical opinion can easily outweigh scientifically determined facts in the eyes of FDA law.

The judge disregarded the views of Dr. Linus Pauling, a Nobel Laureate, Dr. Robert Cathcart who had treated 9,000 patients with large doses of vitamin C, and Irwin Stone who had published 120 papers on vitamin C. Instead the judge relied on the testimony of a pharmacology specialist employed by the California Food and Drug Branch and a physician board certified in internal medicine who merely had to say that mainstream medicine didn't agree.

Klenner debunked the claim that ascorbic acid produces kidney stones as a myth. In fact, it is a good diuretic and produces a pH condition not conducive to oxalate precipitation. In any case, methylene blue, according to Dr. M. J. Vernon Smith, will dissolve calcium oxalate stones if they form. The experience of the Riordan Clinic in Wichita, which has treated thousands of patients with vitamin C infusions, supports Klenner. They are not the kidney stone capital of the world!

Vitamin C, Infectious Diseases and Toxins by Thomas E. Levy, MD, JD is dedicated to Klenner and provides access to documentation showing that Klenner's principles of vitamin C therapy are firmly based in the scientific literature. It contains over 1,200 references. He notes that acute polio and acute hepatitis, two diseases considered incurable by modern medicine, have been consistently cured by vitamin C therapy. Despite the existence of more than 24,000 articles on vitamin C listed in MEDLINE in 2002, the medical establishment continues to ignore this valuable orthomolecular substance. Levy suggests that vaccinations for many viral infectious diseases, like measles, mumps and other diseases of childhood may be unnecessary if one has access to proper dosages of vitamin C.

Only about 10 milligrams per day of vitamin C prevents scurvy, but larger amounts are valuable for many conditions. E. M. Baker, *American Journal of Clinical Nutrition* 20, 583-590 (1927), G. A. Goldsmith, *N.Y. Academy of Science Annals* 92, 230-245 (1961), and R. J. Williams & G. Deason, *Proceeding of the National Academy of Sciences*, USA, 57, 1638-41 (1969) are good research references. Most studies involved animals. There were few human studies, but the animal studies provide conclusive evidence of its functions.

Plants and most animals synthesize their own supplies of vitamin C. It is associated with the germination of seeds and is concentrated in fruits. In animals, it is synthesized from glucose by the liver in 4 enzyme operated steps. Lack of the last enzyme, gulonolactonase, prevents its synthesis in man.

Vitamin C is a powerful reducing agent. In most plants and animals it is the only reducing agent that operates in acid solutions. Its stability is affected by pH, temperature, and traces of copper. Some of it in food is destroyed by cooking. Ascorbic oxidase in fruits and vegetables accelerate oxidation in the presence of oxygen.

The highest concentration in man is found in the retina. Concentrations decrease in the following order: pituitary gland, corpus lueteum, adrenal cortex, liver, brain, testes, ovaries, spleen, thyroid, pancreas and finally erythrocytes in the plasma. Kidneys oxidize vitamin C to a unionized form that is able to penetrate cell barriers. About 5 grams are stored in normal people with adequate diets. Blood plasma contains 0.5 to 2.0 gms. Deprived of new supplies, plasma concentrations drop to 0 in about 2 weeks. Scurvy appears if deprivation continues for about 15 more weeks. None of the vitamin shows up in the urines when concentration in plasma is below 1.4 mg/100 ml.

The need for vitamin C is increased by stress, infections, allergies, lead poisoning, and exposure to low temperatures. It probably plays a role in the functioning of all tissues.

The unstressed rat has been found to produce 70 mg of C per Kg of body weight and the stressed rat 215 mg/Kg. The equivalent amounts for a 150 pound man would be 4.9 to 15 grams. However, not every animal produces or requires the same amount of C. For example, guinea pig requirements for vitamin C vary at least 20 fold. In human terms, a sick older woman in an apartment in New York City can be expected to have different needs for ascorbic acid than a healthy young man on a farm in Iowa!

The pathological syndromes of genetic diseases like phenylketoneuria, galactosemia, and alkatoneuria, which are all caused by the failure of inactive or defective genes to produce important enzymes, affect some of us. But we all were born with hypoascorbemia (the scientific term for the genetic inability to produce vitamin C) first described and named by biochemist Irwin Stone. Most animals including dogs, cats, rats, lions and elephants are capable of internally satisfying their needs for this essential substance, but mankind is not. Vitamin C and sodium ascorbate are safe and effective based on the fact that they are natural components of the immune systems of humans.

Is it possible that the Physician's Union and the drug companies recognized that the need for drugs and medical services might plummet if everyone took adequate amounts of vitamin C? Viral diseases like colds, influenza, pneumonia and many of the diseases of childhood would be less serious and encountered less frequently. That might be a minor threat to the income of physicians, but it would have a marked effect on the sale of medications, and over-the-counter remedies for the treatment of those diseases. In the economic context, it may not be surprising that the medical profession has been adamantly opposed to the idea that vitamin C can cure viral diseases like colds and influenza for years. They have supported this position with a plethora of studies designed to fail - usually by using inadequate amounts of C. But Klenner, who used large amounts of injectable vitamin C in his practice, found that the scientific literature had a large number of studies demonstrating that this vitamin could cure a variety of diseases in the 1940's. There are even more in the scientific literature now.

Vitamin C is cheap and effective. If used by people in optimum quantities, which vary from person to person, it could reduce the cost of medical care. Is this why physicians can lose their licenses to practice medicine by providing vitamin C injections and infusions?

Abram Hoffer stated that in the 1930's and 1940's, physicians were experimenting with newly discovered vitamins but that after 1950 this activity ceased. In that year federal government authorities began promoting the idea that an adequate diet, in accordance with government guidelines, was all that was needed for good health. The recommended daily allowances (RDAs) of vitamins and the food pyramid became the standards for practicing physicians to recommend to their patients. The standard American diet (SAD) was born and the health of Americans began a long decline.

VITAMIN C AND MENTAL DISEASES

Schizophrenic patients need more Vitamin C, and copper than sane people. In 1963, Milner found that 1 gm/D of vitamin C produced significant improvements in schizophrenic patients. Ascorbic Acid and Schizophrenia by Marijan Herjanic provides a great deal of information about vitamin C and ascorbates. Herjanic, in 1966, confirmed that they require twenty to 40 grams for saturation when normal people require only five grams. Some contend that this is due to deficient diet and unknown factors associated with hospitalization. It is known that epinephrine, and nor-epinephrine, are secreted in increased amounts under stress, anxiety, and aggressive reactions. "Almost any disturbance of mind or body will cause significant changes in vitamin C levels in plasma. [21]" Chronically hospitalized schizophrenic patients may require up to 70 grams to reach saturation. Phenothiazines have been found to increase blood levels of C and the greater the increase the greater the clinical improvement.

Respiratory infections and fever sometimes reduce vitamin C levels to 0, and severe exertion also drastically reduces C levels. Both schizophrenics and controls have lower vitamin C levels when anxious than when not.

It is reasonable to believe that those who regularly take grams of ascorbic acid daily should have immune systems better prepared to ward off infectious diseases than those who limit themselves to milligrams. It is true that a good deal will pass through the body to be processed through the kidneys and leave in the urine but not before protecting the urinary tract from infection. Besides, ascorbic acid is relatively cheap. Unfortunately, it is no longer manufactured in this country. Over 90% of the supplemental vitamin C used in America today is being imported from China. The Chinese military, the PLA, reportedly controls the amount allowed to be exported. This may have national defense and health implications for Americans.

---

21 Baker 1967, Urbach et. al. 1952.

VITAMIN D-3

In the December 18, 2007, issue of *US News and World Report* Deborah Kotz asked whether a single nutrient that protects against diabetes, tuberculosis, cancer, colds and the flu "Sounds too good to be true?" Her article was one of many which followed a sudden flood of research on the beneficial results of vitamin D (D-3) which appeared in prestigious scientific journals like *Science*. Ms. Kotz question may require more research for a definitive answer, but there is no doubt that this vitamin is much more important to everybody's health than previously believed. People in northern climes need to know more about it and take adequate amounts of it.

Dr. Kristine Koski suggested, in an article in the *Canadian Journal of Medicine*, that D-3 is not really a vitamin, but a preprohormone, part of a complex endocrine system that begins with the skin. Much of this system is unknown territory including the amount of D-3 needed for human development, growth and health. For many years, the American Academy of Sciences' Food and Nutrition Board has recommended a daily allowance of 400 international units (IU). This amount shows up on the labels of most one-a-day vitamin bottles. But recent research provides good reason to believe that this substantially underestimates real needs. Those who seem to be at the cutting edge say that we need at least 10 times as much. Dr. David William's November 2008 *Alternatives* news letter suggests 1,000 IU/day for breast fed infants, 600/day for bottle fed infants, and 1,000 IU/day for each 25 pounds of body weight of older children. These levels were said to be consistent with the recommendations of the Vitamin D Council. In 2010, the Life Extension Foundation recommended 7,000 IU per day for adults. Toxicity was reported to be at 40,000 IU/d a few years ago, but recently 100,000 IU/d was mentioned as a possible new limit.

Low maternal intakes of this "vitamin" may have long term implications. It has been found that it affects birth weight, fetal skeletal formation, immune function, and chronic disease susceptibility (CMAJ 4/25/06). Japanese researchers have found that a soft spot on the top of the head of newborn babies, called craniotabes is caused by inadequate vitamin D intake during pregnancy. This condition increases the probability of numerous health problems during infancy such as pediatric cardiomyopathy and asthma.

Milk intake by pregnant women has also been found to have a significant effect on birth weight. In a Canadian study, each additional cup of milk increased infant birth weight by an average of 41 grams. And milk contains the less potent vitamin D-2, an artificial analog of the real vitamin.

Exposure of hands and face to the sun for 15 minutes a day is supposed to convert enough 7-dehydrocholecalciferol to activated D-3 for the average person. However, this requires the sun to provide the proper ultra-violet wavelengths. Exposure to the sun in

Boston, Massachusetts, USA and in Edmonton in Canada doesn't always provide D-3. The closer people are to the poles, the more they are likely to be deficient in this important nutriment. (Webb AR et. al. *Jl. of Clinical Endocrine Medicine,* 1988) and Horlick, MF *Am. Jl. Of Clinical Nutrition,* 1995). Furthermore, it takes up to 24 hours for the D-3 produced on your skin by the sun to be absorbed into your body. Thus, a shower right after a sunbath washes off any vitamin D-3 on the skin.

The January 2007 issue of *Health Hunters,* a publication of the Center for the Improvement of Human Functioning International, reports that John Cannel, MD, a psychiatrist at California's Atascadero State Hospital, found that the ward he supervised was free of influenza although surrounded by wards quarantined because of a virulent strain. He had prescribed high doses of vitamin D for the patients in his ward. The explanation may be contained in a paper published in the *FASEB Journal* a few months after the event. It stated that vitamin D increases production of antimicrobial compounds in white blood cells. A compound called cathelicidin may have protected Dr. Cannel's patients from the influenza virus. This is said to punch holes in microbes as part of immune system activity.

Dr. Robert P. Heaney of Creighton University believes that large doses of D-3 could substantially reduce hip fractures, the incidence of a number of cancers, and several autoimmune diseases. (*Journal of Steroid Biochemistry& Molecular Biology,* Jan, 9, 2007.) He is joined by Cedric F Garland of University of California at San Diego who suggests that the present cancer death rates might be substantially reduced. Heart disease could also be helped. Dr. Armin Zittmann, PhD, of the Northrhine Westphalia Heart Center in Germany notes that low levels of this substance encourages calcification of arteries which doesn't happen with higher concentrations until more than 100,000 IU per day is ingested. A Japanese study indicates 70% reduced risk of death from heart disease could accompany substantially increased intake of this vitamin.

It is also possible that vitamin D, by energizing the immune system, increases the effectiveness of vitamin C and other substances which are known to play important roles in both the prevention and cure of many diseases. In particular, vitamin C is one of the few antiviral substances. Synergy between these two vitamins, in my opinion, provides a more satisfying explanation of Dr. Cannell's experience than the assumption that vitamin D, by itself, has antiviral properties.

The Life Extension Foundation has been recommending supplementation with vitamin D-3 for years. Numerous studies show that deficiency in this vitamin is pervasive among Americans. Others show that a substantial number of lives could be saved by adequate supplementation with it. According to John Cannell, MD, founder of the Vitamin D Council, "Current research indicates vitamin D deficiency plays a role in causing 17 varieties of cancer as well as heart disease, stroke, hypertension, autoimmune diseases, diabetes, depression, chronic pain, osteoarthritis, osteoporosis, muscle weakness, birth defects, and periodontal disease."

A recent study revealed that men with high levels of vitamin D-3 in their blood substantially reduced their chances of a coronary artery disease heart attack. According to this study, 92,500 of the 157,000 men who die every year from this disease could be saved by adequate vitamin D-3 supplementation. Deaths from all kinds of heart disease total 869,700 per year. It is reasonable to believe that a substantial number of these deaths can also be averted by judicious use of this vitamin. According to the American Heart Association, 920,000 heart attacks occur yearly. The associated costs amount to $156 billion. If only 50% of them can be averted, $75 billion in yearly savings could be achieved with the expenditure of about $7 billion to supply all 300 million Americans with 1000 IU of vitamin D-3 per day.

There is no doubt that vitamin D-3 helps prevent many cancers. Each year about 190,000 women receive a breast cancer diagnosis and about 41,000 are killed by their disease. Studies indicate that the incidence of breast cancer can be reduced by 30 to 50% with adequate vitamin D-3 supplementation. About 190,000 men get a prostate cancer diagnosis each year and 30,000 are killed by the disease. Men with high blood levels of vitamin D-3 have a 52% reduction in incidence. Similarly, 145,000 Americans get colon cancer every year and the disease kills about 53,000 of them. It has been estimated that 38,000 colon cancer deaths could be averted and at least $5 billion saved yearly if everyone received enough vitamin D-3.

For the last 40 years, costs of cancer have been about 4½% of total health care costs. In 2007, these costs totaled $78 billion. It is not unreasonable to believe that proper supplementation of the entire population with vitamin D-3 could save $ billions a year.

Estimated direct and indirect costs of stroke in 2010, according to the CDC, are $76.6 billion. In September, 2008, a study published in *Stroke* stated that low concentrations of vitamin D-3 in the blood were "independently predictive for fatal strokes." Since strokes are averted by monitoring D-3 in patient's blood, additional billions might be saved.

Unfortunately, most physicians are trained to recognize vitamin D-3 deficiencies at levels of 12 nanograms per milliliter (ngm/ml) where rickets develop in children, and adults get osteomalacia. Nutrition experts consider 50 ng/ml as optimum and many laboratory reference ranges classify 32 ng/ml as deficient. Wouldn't it be economically worthwhile to modernize the Standards of Care with respect to vitamin deficiencies when possible savings exceeding billions of dollars a year are involved?

In 2007, William Faloon, editor of *Life Extension* magazine, urged the Federal Government to accept 50,000 bottles, each containing a year's supply of the vitamin, for distribution to Medicare patients who couldn't afford to buy them. He did this in a good will effort to help reduce the cost of health care. To date this offer has been ignored. Does this mean that the Federal Government is not interested in saving money?

SODIUM CHLORITE

Sodium chlorite has been used to purify drinking water for many years. Acidified sodium chlorite is also presently approved by the FDA for sanitizing meat in the meat packing industry, to rid eggs of pathogens, and to sanitize vegetables. It is regulated by the Environmental Protection Agency. Under the proper conditions it can be converted into chlorine dioxide. Jim Humble claims it is a powerful immune system enhancer because of its anti-pathogenic properties.

The book Breakthrough by Jim Humble, a retired scientist and gold prospector, describes the research that led him to believe that minute amounts of acidified sodium chlorite could be effective against malaria. He encountered this disease frequently while searching for gold in South American jungles. Mr. Humble states that tests at several locations in Africa showed that it could quickly dispose of the malaria parasite. He also now claims that is has been used successfully to treat AIDS in Africa. His research and reports from users lead Humble to believe that this substance is effective against any disease which the immune system can subdue. He has established a worldwide mission and following to promote MMS as an alternative health modality.

As of this writing there appears to be an extensive controversy about the merits of acidified sodium chlorite. Physicians, alternative health practitioners, chemists and lay people are studying the benefits and risks of using MMS both internally and externally. From internet reports and the number of web sites on MMS, it is believed that thousands of people worldwide are experimenting with MMS. Health benefit claims vary and there are physicians and researchers who are adamantly stating that MMS is dangerous and should not be used internally under any condition. There has been one reported death claimed from the use of MMS.

The MMS controversy, however it is resolved, illustrates how freedom of choice in medical care and independent research may be the quickest way for the public to determine what claims are true. What is now happening is that physicians, chemists, and other credentialed researchers, are taking various positions on the use (or not) of MMS in an open forum. Instead of years of testing and expensive double blind studies that still could illicit conflicting results, people around the world can now read on the Internet what the advocates and detractors of MMS claim. In a free society it should be up to individuals to determine if they want to try MMS for a medical condition or an alternate modality.

Note that the FDA issued a health "Warning Notice" to users of MMS in July 2010 and advised against drinking MMS in any form for the treatment of any condition.

SILVER

A raft of articles and books on colloidal silver have recently appeared accompanied by newsletters and advertisements by both producers of colloidal silver and manufacturers of devices for producing varieties of it. According to <u>Colloidal Silver: A Closer Look</u> by Peter A. Lindemann, most health food stores carry this product and there are several sources of generators for making it at home. There are said to be millions of satisfied users of colloidal silver.

Lindemann says that there are at least 4 different products being called colloidal silver. The first is called electro-colloidal silver and is made by one of 2 methods: Either by low voltage electrolysis in distilled water or with an electric arc in deionized water. The second is called mild silver protein, and involves chemically binding silver particles to a protein. The third variety is silver salts, produced either chemically or electrically. The fourth is powdered silver, developed by Russians, which involves silver dust produced by high voltage discharge through a silver wire and dispersed in water. All are said to work, but there are no industry or government regulations controlling quality. Quality can vary from batch to batch. A light yellow color is said to be associated with products of good quality.

Erick Rentz, DO, in an interview with Greg Ciola, Editor of the *Crusador*, indicated that a new product, silver hydrosol, was superior to most colloidal silver products because over 90% of the particles carried a negative charge versus for 8 to 35% in the case of other products. He said that 1 drop of this preparation in a glass of water or fruit juice would kill any pathogens in a short period of time. Two teaspoon full's swished around the mouth a few times and swallowed every 15 minutes for one hour and once every hour for the rest of the day, if repeated for two more days could help alleviate an impending herpes outbreak.

The Institute of Microbiology in Rome, Italy, tested a number of silver containing products for their ability to kill micro-organisms. They concluded that pure colloidal silver was superior to both silver salts and sulfadiazine in killing the bacteria, fungus, and mold samples tested. Additives reduced the effectiveness of the pure product. The study was published in *Applied and Environmental Microbiology* in 1992. The effectiveness as a broad spectrum germicide has been found to depend on particle size and stability. Smaller particles tend to be more effective than larger ones.

Silver can act as a toxic heavy metal producing a condition called Argyria, evidenced as a permanent bluish condition of the skin. It can also produce a wide range of symptoms as recorded in the <u>Homeopathic Materia Medica</u>. On the other hand, it can provide many benefits when used as a trace mineral nutriment. For example, according to reports, it can kill a wide range of micro-organisms. *JAMA* articles have warned against Argyria, and toxicity of colloidal silver. The

Food and Drug Administration have labeling guidelines, and some believe, a lot of data on safety and effectiveness which has not being published.

In the 1940 *Journal of Nutrition* R.A. Kehoe reported that the average daily intake of silver from dietary sources was 50 to 100 micrograms (mcg) per day. Since farming has been depleting our soils of minerals for 70 years since then, very little silver is left in the standard American diet. The 1992, Earth Summit *Report* stated that levels of minerals in our soils had dropped 85% in the previous 100 years. Reports indicate that 2 to 4 teaspoonfuls of 5 ppm colloidal silver containing about 50 to 100 mcg of silver may be safe to take on a daily basis as a dietary supplement. Of course you should always consult your health care provider before embarking on a new therapy.

CHAPTER 6 - MENTAL DISEASES

According to the National Institutes of Health 26.2% of Americans, 57.7 million of us aged 18 or over, suffer from a diagnosable mental disorder. Mental Health Statistics, a website operated by John Drohol, PsyD states that 32.4% of us are crazy at any one time, and the lifetime prevalence is 57.4%. Are we approaching the point where we can say, like the mythical old Quaker: "Everyone is a little queer but thee and me – and sometimes thee?" Or are psychiatrists seeking more customers for their psychoactive drugs?

There has been a notable expansion in the number of new mental diseases listed in the <u>Diagnostic and Statistical Manual of Mental Disorders</u> recently. Teenagers and college students with emotional problems incident to the change from child to adult have been targets. College students who smoke or drink are now considered to have a mental disease. Psychoactive drugs fed to school children, many with autism and other brain damage, which many people believe are the result of the national immunization program, may be creating some of the new diseases.

Serious mental diseases like schizophrenia, and bipolar disease, by some estimates, affect 2.6% and 2.4% of us respectively for a total of 5% of the population. However, the NIMH estimates that only 1% of

Americans are schizophrenic. The disease is said to be incurable and the cause unknown. Victims can only have their symptoms controlled by psychoactive drugs.

SCHIZOPHRENIA

For some thirty years, schizophrenia was considered to be a result of hyperactive production of the neurotransmitter dopamine, and the resultant effects on the brain. More recently, neuroscientists have concluded that it isn't quite that simple. Dr. Nancy Andreason, head of the psychiatry department at the University of Iowa College of Medicine, wrote in 2003, that "Clinician scientists now think that schizophrenia occurs as a consequence of a much more complex chemical imbalance that includes multiple neurotransmitter systems that interact with and modulate one another."

Patients afflicted with schizophrenia have a disease which affects the whole body. It has both physical and mental symptoms. It is a disease in which reality is perceived abnormally by the sense organs of patients. It is curable. The natural cure rate, without medical intervention, is 50% as noted by John Connolly in his lecture to the Royal College of Physicians in London in 1849. In the 1840's, the Quaker asylum near Philadelphia was able to release 45% of its mental patients back into society as cured and 25% more as improved using "moral treatment"- good food, a safe environment, and civility.

In the 1950's, Drs. Abram Hoffer and Humphrey Osmund identified the probable cause of schizophrenia as the production of LSD-like molecules in the brain. Their double blind tests showed that over 75% of schizophrenic patients were curable with a combination of psychiatric treatments and adequate amounts of vitamin C, B-3, and B-6. Hoffer, the Father of Orthomolecular Psychiatry and President of the Canadian Schizophrenic Association, now deceased, claimed that he turned 5,000 schizophrenic patients into taxpayers. He also claimed that 95% of schizophrenic patients are curable if they get orthomolecular psychiatric treatment soon after the disease appears. In contrast, an American psychiatrist is reported to have testified in court that he treated 10,000 such patient and cured none of them. Why do so few American schizophrenic patients recover to become taxpayers?

In the preface to his book Mad in America, published in 2002, Robert Whitaker, a medical journalist, notes that the World Health Organization [WHO] has been puzzled by the fact that schizophrenia outcomes in the United States and other developed countries are much worse than those in the poor countries of the world. In India and Nigeria, he reports, those suffering psychotic incidents have a good chance of recovering in a couple of years. In the United States, they are likely to become chronically ill. There is an important clue to a probable explanation for the difference contained in the WHO statistics published in *Psychological Medicine*, supplement 20, in 1992. In developed countries, during the follow-up period after hospital discharge, most patients were on antipsychotic medications and few such patients were on these medications in the developing countries.

Research by Courtney Harding, a psychologist at the University of Colorado, reported in 1957, long term outcomes of 82 schizophrenics discharged in the 1950's from Vermont State Hospital. She found that 33% had recovered completely. They had all successfully weaned themselves off of neuroleptic medications prescribed by their psychiatrists. She concluded that the idea that schizophrenics needed to stay on medications for the rest of their lives is a myth.

There are more than 2 million schizophrenics in this country, and too many end up in prison, homeless, or shuttling in and out of psychiatric hospitals. Annual costs are about $50 billion. Whitaker claims that there has been a long term decline in outcomes and we are back where we were almost 80 years ago when the insane were left for hours or, sometimes days, trussed up in wet sheets as a physiologically beneficial treatment for "restlessness."

Mad in America presents a disturbing picture of American psychiatry and its treatment of the insane. In contrast Orthomolecular Psychiatry, edited by David Hawkins and Linus Pauling in 1973, offers the promise of more humane, scientifically based treatments for schizophrenia which, if fully exploited should permit a substantially better outlook for patients and lower costs to society. The premise of this book is that mental diseases are diseases of the brain and that the brain itself needs to be treated by changing its molecular composition.

VITAMIN B-3

Early in the last century about 10% of the patients in mental hospitals were suffering from pellagra, a vitamin deficiency disease. In 1937, medical scientists discovered that about 12 milligrams per day of niacin, vitamin B-3, prevented pellagra. This discovery led to investigations of this vitamin's utility in the treatment of other mental conditions. Moderately large doses of B-3 were found to improve the condition of patients with a variety of acute mental illnesses. In 1943, William Kauffman, MD, described a disease which he called aniacinamidosis which involved deterioration in mental and physical health. He found that patients taking 1 to 5 grams per day (g/d) of niacinamide improved their mental and physical health and also the mobility of their joints. The father of medicine, Hippocrates of Cos, suggested that we should let food be our medicine didn't he?

In 1952, Abram Hoffer, MD, PhD, and Humphrey Osmond, MRCP & FRCP of Tuscaloosa, Alabama, began the first double blind trial of niacin and niacinamide (vitamin B-3) for the treatment of schizophrenia in Saskatchewan, Canada. It was highly successful and confirmed previous indication that this orthomolecular treatment for mental disease worked surprisingly well. Subsequent experiments by Hoffer, et. al., in 1957 and 1962, and by Denson in 1962, provided convincing evidence that patients who took the vitamin, in addition to other treatments, did better than those who did not. Since there were only about 1 million people in Saskatchewan at that time, and the record keeping system was unusually efficient, Hoffer and Osmund were able to follow the progress of their patients for as long as 15 years even with limited resources.

Ultimately, their orthomolecular treatment of schizophrenics involved 3 to 6 grams per day (g/d) of ascorbic acid, 600 to 1500 milligrams per day (mg/d) of pyridoxine, and sometimes over 6 g/d of niacin or niacinamide. With substantial proof of the efficacy of their cheap, safe, and easy therapy, one might expect that psychiatrists would have welcomed this advancement in medical science with open arms. Nothing could be further from the truth. Their findings were greeted with disbelief instead and, to this day, are little used. Evidently the discovery and promotion of the first antipsychotic drug was more important to psychiatrists and focused their attention and interest.

In 1951, French naval surgeon, Henri Laborit, tested chlorpromazine on surgical patients and found that he could perform operations on them with almost no anesthesia. European physicians had found that patients on the drug became immobile and could be moved around like puppies. This result was similar to that achieved by lobotomy used by psychiatrists to gain control of difficult patients in mental hospitals at that time.

THORAZINE

Penicillin seemed to be the solution for infectious diseases. An equivalent solution for mental diseases might be at hand. After obtaining the rights to market chlorpromazine in the United States from Rhone-Poulenc in the spring of 1952, Smith, Klein and French spent about $350,000 on its development. In a hurry to market the drug, they tested it on about 150 psychiatric patients as an anti-emetic and applied for FDA approval. The FDA approved it as an anti-emetic on March 2, 1954, and the product, now named thorazine, was launched soon after that with a national television show called "The March of Medicine." Francis Boyer, president of Smith, Klein & French, told the public that the product had been tested on 50,000 animals and then evaluated by 2,000 physicians in the US and Canada.

To ensure budgetary support for its market, the company set up a task force to coach hospital administrators and psychiatrists in every state on what to say to state legislators to convince them that the drug would save taxpayers money and restore lives of patients. It was a well conceived program that won acceptance for the drug. As it proceeded, thorazine was transformed from an anti-emetic to a chemical lobotomist, and finally into a means for returning hopeless psychotics to normal.

American and Canada mental health professionals welcomed thorazine because, unlike most other therapies such as barbiturates, bromides, chloral, paraldehyde, hydrotherapy, electroshock, metrazole shock, histamine shock, insulin shock, and lobotomy, it acted quickly. One injection could turn a violent patient into the equivalent of a puppy. Unfortunately, many patients, kept out of hospitals by its use, wound up chronically disabled.

With use, thorazine's undesirable side effects were discovered. Swiss psychiatrist Hans Stack reported that 37% of 399 patients treated with thorazine showed signs of Parkinson's disease. In 1954, England's Joel Elkins reported that schizophrenic and paraphrenic patients taking the drug continued to have delusions and hallucinations, but were less disturbed by them. Nevertheless, by some magical process, according to Edward Shorter's 1997 book A History of Psychiatry, thorazine was claimed able to permit schizophrenics to lead normal lives and not be confined to institutions. This opened the way for governments to move mental patients out of insane asylums and reduce their already parsimonious support of these institutions.

Recognizing that their achievements were not receiving adequate attention in the professional community, Hoffer and Osmund published How to Live with Schizophrenia. Subsequently the popular press, and radio, and TV pundits joined in praising the use of niacin for schizophrenia as a new discovery. As a result, the National Institute of Mental Health investigated and provided a substantial grant for a 3 year study of the use of niacin in the treatment of schizophrenia. Psychiatrists complained that their patients had information about niacin before they did, but had only themselves to blame for not keeping up with the scientific literature. The fact that niacin is not listed in Robert Whitaker's book's index indicates that important advances in medical science, even if they receive the attention of the press, are easily sidetracked and buried by a medical establishment intent on serving its own interests.

In the affluent and exuberant 1920's this country experienced a surge of interest in drugs like opium, marijuana, cocaine, and alcohol. The demon rum, at that time, held center stage and flappers, the female examples of exuberant youth, smoked cigarettes, drank alcohol and wore very short skirts to emphasize rebellion against established authority. When the Federal Reserve Bank put an end to the exuberance in 1929 by sterilizing the large inflows of European gold, which could have supported the stock market bonanza, the party ended for most people. A great many families didn't have enough money to put food on the table. Few people could afford opium, which the English distributed as products of India, and few people knew that the Mexican laborers, who helped build our railroads, had planted marijuana along the tracks. The incipient drug culture, except for alcohol, withered. Due to the effects of Prohibition, which made manufacture, sale, and use of alcohol for recreational purposes, illegal, gangsters monopolized the high gross margin business of supplying it to those who could afford the price.

After World War II, another affluent society spawned hippies instead of flappers and the drug scene expanded into academia where Timothy Leary proposed that people should "turn on and drop out." Chemical research on new drugs provided choices unavailable to previous generations. Among them was LSD, which opened the way for experimental youth to experience changes in perception of reality used from time immemorial by native shamans for religious ceremonies in many primitive countries. The "War on Drugs" again served to generate a high margin business monopolized by gangsters. But this time use of drug trade profits to finance French intelligence operations during the Vietnamese War introduced a sinister connection between the gangsters and a government. There are hints that such connections may have transferred to our own military intelligence operations when French influence waned in Vietnam.

Academic research on LSD led to the recognition that it was producing mind bending experiences in users which were believed to be similar to those which plagued schizophrenics. This may have influenced the search for evidence of a psychoactive molecule which might be causing schizophrenia. In 1954, Dr. Hoffer suggested that a derivative of adrenaline, called adenochrome, might be involved.

Paul Hoch, MD, of German descent, born in Budapest and trained in Europe, became a national leader in schizophrenia research as director of the Department of Experimental Psychiatry at the New York State Psychiatric Institute. He tested mescaline and LSD on about 60 mental patients between 1949 and 1952. He reported that both drugs heightened the schizophrenic disorganization of the individual. In addition, these substances could trigger full-blown schizophrenic episodes in patients who did not display many signs of schizophrenic thinking. One of his case studies involved a 36 year old man who had simply complained of constant tension, social inadequacy, and inability to relax. Under the influence of mescaline symptoms of schizophrenia were observed. The patient saw dragons and tigers coming to eat him and reacted to these hallucinations with marked anxiety. After being treated to a transorbital lobotomy and again given mescaline, similar manifestations occurred, but the symptoms were not as severe.

Hoch was appointed commissioner of New York's mental health department and was elected president of the Society of Biological Psychiatry. The New York State Psychiatric Institute holds a bronze plaque hailing him as a compassionate physician, original researcher, and dedicated scientist. The ethics of his experiments do not seem to have been questioned.

In 1962, Leo Hollister, a Veterans Administration psychiatrist critiqued the use of psychedelic drugs in research, noting that schizophrenics experienced mostly auditory rather than visual hallucinations. When possession and sale of these drugs became illegal in the 1960s, NIMH grants for Hoch's kind of research dried up.

It is interesting to contrast Dr. Hoch's high technology treatment of mental patients to that of Dr. Thomas Kirkbride, a Quaker physician, graduate of the University of Pennsylvania who did his residency at the Friends Asylum in Frankford. He ran a new asylum opened near Philadelphia in 1841 using a system developed by the Quakers called "moral treatment." Patients were roused at 6 AM, exercised daily in the gymnasium, attended classes in reading or sewing, had access to a library with 1,100 volumes and enjoyed evening entertainments including lectures, concerts, and theatrical performances. Kirkbride encouraged patients to develop friendships, dress well, rethink their behavior, acknowledge that they had behaved badly, and should reestablish ties with their families. He carefully selected attendants for qualities including patience, coolness, and courage; provided them with rule books, and fired any who hit a patient. The record shows that of 8,546 patients admitted to his asylum between 1841 and 1882, 45% were discharged as cured and 25% as improved. Apparently the Quakers religious belief that love and empathy had restorative power, the basis for "moral treatment," worked.

Unfortunately, a successful reformer, Dorethea Dix, who had suffered a breakdown and recovered in England via "moral treatment," initiated a revolution. She convinced a number of state legislatures to establish asylums for the "moral treatment" of their insane. Parsimonious politicians prevented the public facilities from matching the Quaker standards and an unmanageable mixture of patients, in addition to the newly insane, overloaded the underfinanced new asylums. Wages were low and the staffs, recruited from the lowest rungs of society were not inclined to treat noxious patients with kindness. Charity boards set up by legislatures to manage asylums, faced with budgetary problems, actively opposed expensive "moral treatment." The asylums quickly became overloaded with chronic patients. Many had terminal illnesses like syphilis. The asylums were ripe for a change in management.

Coming to the rescue were a horde of neurologists who had gained expertise treating wounded soldiers during the Civil War. The already harried superintendents of the state asylums, mostly appointed bureaucrats, were no match for the neurologists. They accepted defeat in 1892. The Quakers' backlash against harsh treatments of psychotic patients ended at the turn of the century. The patients in their asylums were turned over to the tender mercies of practitioners of "scientific medicine."

One field of science which had an important impact on the treatment of the insane was eugenics.

Initiated by Francis Galton, a cousin of Charles Darwin, who coined the word in 1883, it proposed to promote the reproduction of superior humans and discourage the reproduction of defectives. The severely mentally ill were believed to have inferior germ plasma and their reproduction was to be discouraged. The new science was much debated in England but it received its first implementation in the US. Funded by Andrew Carnegie, John D. Rockefeller, and Mary Harriman, and championed by the Ivy League universities, its proponents fostered the enactment of laws for compulsory sterilization of the mentally ill and other unfit members of society.

Harvard University's Earnest Hooten suggested that the insane really ought to be exterminated. Nobel Prize winner, Dr. Alexis Carrel at the Rockefeller Institute of Medical Research suggested, in his 1935 book Man the Unknown that the insane, or at least those who had committed any sort of crime, should be humanely and economically disposed of in small euthanasia institution supplied with proper gases. In 1940, Germany undertook the task of ridding itself of its mental patients with "proper gases." Adolph Hitler, influenced by what he called his bible, The Passing of the Great Race, by Madison Grant, founder of the American Eugenics Society, took Dr. Carrel's suggestion and eliminated over 70,000 mental patients.

A modern trial of the Quakers' "moral treatment" concept occurred in the 1970's when Loren Mosher, MD, Director of the Center for Schizophrenia studies at the National Institute of Mental Health (NIMH), obtained a $150,000 grant for support of the Soteria project for 2 years. Located in Santa Clara, California the project opened in a 12 room house in 1971 with 6 resident patients. They were young, unmarried, acutely ill schizophrenics expected to have poor outcomes. The staff was specially chosen with social skills capable of coping with their strange, annoying, and threatening charges. There were no locks on the doors, no seclusion rooms, no wet packs, no drugs. Treated like human beings, and given food, respect, and understanding in a loving atmosphere, residents recovered. In 1974, Mosher published data showed that, at 6 weeks, psychotic symptoms of the Soteria patient abated to the same degree as medicated patients. Furthermore, they stayed well longer; their relapse rates were better; and they were better able to hold a job or attend school than medicated patients. That publication marked the beginning of the end of Mosher' career at the NIMH.

Mosher initially had asked for $700,000 to support a 7 year trial. The Clinical Projects Research Review Committee, composed of leading academic psychiatrists, controlled funding. They were not happy about this project because it might prove that ordinary people could help psychotics as well as highly educated psychiatrists. They approved only $150,000 for a 2 year trial. In 1973, they only approved $50,000 per year, an obvious kiss of death. However, Mosher was able to make an end-run; obtaining $500,000 for 5 year support of a second Soteria project named Emanon, from another division of the NIMH involved with social services for the mentally ill.

Out maneuvered on funding, the eminent psychiatrists changed their strategy. After Mosher published results, they charged that the study had serious flaws and the evidence of outcomes was "not compelling." The final blow was the statement that they would approve further funding only if Mosher was replaced by another investigator who would work with the committee to redesign the experiment. Mosher was branded as anti-science because he hadn't used the neuroleptics (mind altering drugs) which mainstream psychiatry depended upon. His position at NIMH was given to one of his assistants in 1980, and he was transferred to Bethesda, Maryland, to train psychiatrists for service in the military. Subsequently he resigned from the American Psychiatric Association. His letter of resignation, which can be found on the internet, makes interesting reading. [22] In it he says that he believes he is actually resigning from the 'American Psychopharmacological Association' which condones and promotes "the widespread use and overuse of toxic chemicals that we know have serious long term effects."

Mosher's projects were so under funded and otherwise hobbled that none of their results were published and their data wasn't even analyzed for 20

---

22 See Appendix 3.

years. Recently, John Bola, assistant professor at the University of Southern California analyzed all of the data and found that the results were even better than Mosher had indicated in 1974. Only 31% of Soteria patients relapsed after 2 years compared with 68% relapses for patients treated conventionally with neuroleptics. Relapse rates were high, however, for Soteria patients who were put on neuroleptics by their psychiatrists after they left Soteria.

While American psychiatrists were busy forgetting Mosher's experiment, Swiss researchers were replicating it. In 1992, they reported that patients who received no, or very low, doses of medication fared significantly better than those who received conventional therapy. Two-thirds of their Soteria patients had favorable outcomes mirroring Mosher's experience. The Swedes and Finns have invested in Soteria houses and have reported good outcomes using psychosocial programs with minimal usage of neuroleptics.

The fact that outcomes for schizophrenics are better in undeveloped countries than in our country makes it reasonable to believe that there is room for substantial improvement in the way patients are treated by American psychiatrists. The fact that Mosher's Soteria experiment appears to have been successful despite the efforts of eminent academic psychiatrists to ham-string it, indicates that it is not safe to leave control of research funds in the hands of those with economic interests in outcomes.

167

The fact that the Swedes and Finns are getting the benefits of research results distained by distinguished American academic psychiatrist merits a Congressional investigation of public expenditures on medical research. But, unfortunately, Congress established the legal basis for the existing medical monopoly which is causing the problems and is unlikely to want to change laws that have been in place for almost a century.

BIPOLAR DISEASE

According to Dr. Hoffer, psychiatrists used to think that schizophrenia and bipolar disease were different, but apparently it is possible to cure bipolar disease with some of the same orthomolecular therapies that work for schizophrenia. This permits some very talented people with bipolar disease to retain their capabilities instead of losing them to psychoactive drugs.

Past history, as chronicled by Kay Jamison's Touched With Fire shows that a majority of great poets led troubled lives. The divine madness that fed their creativity, went out of control, and damaged their minds. In modern medical terms they suffered from bipolar or manic-depressive disease. Many of them committed suicide. Others wound up in insane asylums or jails. Some talented individuals, believed to have been bipolar, like Alexander the Great, Peter the Great, and Napoleon Bonaparte won their places in history books with outstanding accomplishments despite their disease. In modern times, Richard Branson of Virgin Airlines fame is accomplishing great things despite reported problems with the disease.

Most physicians offer bipolar patients medications which often eliminate the risks associated with the disease but at the price of loss of their creativity and acceptance of undesirable side effects. Fortunately, there is now an alternative. Psychiatrists trained in Orthomolecular Medicine know that bipolar disease has a biochemical cause. It can be cured with modern psychiatric practices, small amounts of drugs and natural substances, like vitamins. Their patients do not have to lose their creativity.

Unfortunately, governments and insurance companies are not inclined pay for orthomolecular treatments. There are no numbers in the six digit AMA copyrighted code that controls payments for medical services for orthomolecular psychiatric treatments. Moreover, there aren't many physicians trained in this discipline so you will have to seek them out.

The International Society of Orthomolecular Medicine at 16 Florence Ave. in Toronto M2N 1E9, Ontario, Canada, can help locate physicians with this training.

EMPOWERPLUS

Several years ago in Canada a product, originally designed to cure ear and tail biting syndrome

169

of pigs, was modified by a biologist to suppress the symptoms of bipolar disease. Although it does not cure this disease, because patients who stop taking the product reacquire bipolar symptoms, it permits a quality of life far superior to that afforded by lithium and other psychoactive drugs. Unfortunately, it does nothing for schizophrenia.

Empowerplus, manufactured and sold by the Truehope Company in Canada, contains 14 vitamins, 16 minerals, 3 amino acids and 3 botanicals. One of the minerals, germanium, is the subject of a book by Kazuhiko Asai, PhD, who discovered it in Japanese's coal and subsequently found that it had many uses in medicine. He claimed that it helped oxygenate the brain.

Dr. Bonnie Kaplan, a psychologist, has conducted preliminary trials at the University of Calgary. She observed significant reductions in symptoms in 12 patients. Many of them stopped taking the supplement briefly and relapsed. She has obtained approval for trials in Calgary and San Diego. Dr. Estelle Goldstein, a psycho-pharmacologist and psychiatrist in San Diego, who uses the product in her practice, is participating in Kaplan's trial.

Dr. Charles Popper, a psycho-pharmacologist at Harvard Medical School, after attending a seminar on Dr. Kaplan's experience with the supplement, found that it worked on a colleague's child who had terrible tantrums. Subsequently, he tried it on other patients and found that a high percentage of them benefited and many were able to substitute the supplement for their psychotropic drugs.

More than 10,000 bipolar patients are said to have benefited by using this product. Each is considered to be an anecdotal case. Establishment medicine requires double blind studies to make sure that the "placebo effect" is not causing the benefits. Practically speaking, 10,000 successful applications, with no major problems, ought to be enough proof for reasonable people.

In any case, a judge of the Alberta Provincial Court prevented Health Canada (Canada's equivalent of the Department of Health and Human Services) from putting an end to Empowerplus by charging the company with violations of the Canadian Food and Drug Act. He ruled that the defendants were overwhelmingly compelled to disobey the regulations in order to protect the health, safety, and wellbeing of users of the supplement. It is refreshing to have a judge be more concerned for suffering patients than for the medical industrial monopoly which is as active in Canada as it is in the United States.

Empowerplus is available in Canadian health food stores and also on the internet. Bipolar patients on psychoactive medications who wish to try this product should be aware that getting off their drugs will not be easy. People who tried the "cold turkey" route have encountered serious problems. Getting help from a medical professional is recommended

RECOVERY FROM MENTAL DISEASES

Abram Hoffer claimed that only about 10% of American schizophrenics recover to become taxpaying citizens. It is said that those who recovered managed to wean themselves off the drugs their psychiatrists prescribed before too much damage occurred. Wouldn't it be sensible for the American Psychiatric Association members to follow Hoffer's lead and start turning their patients into taxpayers instead of wards of the state? Florida, in 2007, paid $250 million to house mental patients in jails and another $72 million to build more jail cells for them. New York is said to have spent $600 million to keep the mentally ill in flop houses.

NIH literature indicates that 60% of schizophrenics and 80% of bipolar disease patients recover. This is inconsistent with other sources of information, like the NIMH which says these diseases are incurable, and the WHO and the American Psychiatric Association which paint an entirely different picture. Evidently, different definitions of the word "recover" are involved. It is highly unlikely that these percentages of patients are leading productive lives and paying taxes like Dr. Hoffer's patients. Is the NIH trying to white wash the performance of American psychiatrists?

In ancient times, some societies treated the mentally ill with respect because they were considered to be divinely inspired. They are treated with considerable disrespect in America and other countries of the western world. People too easily develop fear of what they do not understand.

RESEARCH

In a 2005 paper on the Internet, *Raising the Bar on Mental Research*, T. R. Insel and T. M. Scolnick note that research on mental disease has not been aimed at cures or prevention and suggest that more creative research in new directions might result in a effective vaccine just as research on poliomyelitis resulted in a vaccine that prevented the disease. Their paper contains a whole page of references, but notably there are no references relating to the six double blind studies that proved that schizophrenics could be cured with orthomolecular psychiatry: the reason being that most papers on this subject have been published in the *Journal of Orthomolecular Medicine*, which <u>MEDLINE</u> has refused to abstract for over 35 years "no matter how good the papers were." Incidentally, several important papers by Nobel Laureate Linus Pauling were published in that Journal which the gatekeepers at MEDLINE are keeping out of sight of their readers. By this means the medical monopoly hopes to keep people who are seriously ill with mental diseases in thrall to the medical monopoly's psychoactive drugs and to induce the public to provide more funds for research to insure profitable employment for its members. It is said that a schizophrenic patient can provide the monopoly between $2 and $4 million over his or her 40 year lifetime.

CHAPTER 7 - MERCURY

In 2009, the *Boston Globe* reported that, according to a CDC study, nearly 1% of American children aged 3 to 17, some 673,000 kids, are autistic. The *New York Times* of Oct. 1, 2004, reported to its readers that the number of children with autism or related diseases in the public school system increased from 118,846 in 2002 to 141,022 in 2003, an increase of 19 percent. It also states that this figure has increased 20% to 25% every year since the mid 1990's. During that time period, more and more people were required to teach these learning-disabled children, adding costs to the public school system, and contributing to the ballooning education budget. A concomitant increase in related diseases, while less severe than full-blown autism, still requires measures aimed at reducing the impact that children who suffer from these disorders can have on the classroom environment. Drugs like Ritalin, widely prescribed for behavior control, also have an impact on other mental functions and do not entirely eliminate disruptive behaviors. Autism has become a plague on our society, devastating families and requiring expensive medical care and special schooling for the innocent victims.

The first cases of autism were reported in 1941 by Dr. Leo Kanner at Johns Hopkins University, and he described the cases of 11 children suffering from extreme autistic aloneness in a medical textbook in 1943. All of those first reported victims were born after 1930 and were autistic at birth. When first identified, autism was considered a birth defect, and was often associated with some degree of mental retardation. Since then, a rise in the number of autistic children with little or no mental retardation has been observed. In 1987, 19% were in this category; today it is 56 percent, and now most infants contract the disease at around 18 months instead of being born with it. In the 1960's, noted psychiatrist Bruno Bettleheim championed Kanner's original hypothesis that autism was caused by "refrigerator mothers" who didn't properly stimulate their children, but that opinion has ultimately not held up. In recent years, autism has come to be considered a neurodevelopmental disorder, rather than a psychiatric one, largely through the research and efforts of the Autism Research Institute.

Dr. Bernard Rimland, founder of the Autism Research Institute, was the father of an autistic child. Born in 1956, he was autistic at birth. Rimland set out to understand his son's condition, and produced a seminal book on the subject of autism in 1964. [23] Although our government's official medical authorities continue to claim that there is no cure for autism, Rimland found that removal of mercury from the bodies of autistic children by use of a special chelating agent improved their condition about 70% of the time. Likewise, those same authorities insist that the cause of this devastating and life-changing disease is still unknown. On the other hand, a growing body of independent physicians and scientists, some with autistic children, have no doubt that the national vaccination program, designed to wipe out childhood diseases, is the probable cause. The program began in 1985 and shortly after, autism

23 Infantile Autism, The Syndrome and Its Implications, 1984.

became a widespread problem.

Another childhood disease in which mercury was implicated was pink disease. The symptoms included pink fingers and toes accompanied by irritability, weakness, sudden and rapid racing of the heart, high blood pressure, photophobia, and inflammation of the peripheral nerves, also known as polyneuritis. One mother is reported to have said, "My child behaves like a mad dog!" It affected babies between six months and two years old in the English-speaking world and two to five years old in Europe. Physicians of that time denied knowledge of the cause of the disease, just as they deny knowing the cause of autism now. Popular theories blamed viruses and nutritional deficiencies, but by 1950 mercury compounds, widely used in teething powders for numbing the gums of teething children, became suspects. The disease disappeared after 1954 when mercury was removed from teething powder.

The Individuals with Disabilities Act was passed in 1975 to ensure equal educational opportunities for disabled children. At that time Congress promised to cover 40% of the costs associated with the program, but it has never funded more than 15% according to Dr. F. E. Yazbak who provides a perspective on autism in the winter 2003 issue of *The Journal of American Physicians and Surgeons*.

Autism, which affects boys more often than girls by a four-to-one ratio, has reached epidemic proportions in the United States. During the 10-year period ending in 2002 there was a 1,700% increase in the number of autistic children in American schools. The total number of disabled children in school increased also, but only by 30%.

177

An autistic child can cost a school system $30,000 a year or more. Since it has been progressively more difficult to fund this program, diagnosis is a serious matter for physicians and not easily approved by school authorities. There are probably more autistic children than the statistics indicate. The rest probably appear under autism-related diseases like Attention Deficit Disorder (ADD) and Attention Deficit Hyperactivity Disorder (ADHD).

At the June 2004 meeting of Doctors for Disaster Preparedness in San Diego, California, Dr. Boyd Haley, Chairman of the Chemistry Department at the University of Kentucky, disclosed that boys are no longer superior to girls in mathematics and science. Boys have also lost about 100 points in test scores. He said affirmative action is needed to get adequate numbers into law and medical school. Haley believes that the probable cause of this reversal in intellectual capabilities is mercury poisoning, which causes something akin to intoxication. He calls it Mad Child Disease.

This disease was "made in America" but is, unfortunately, no longer confined to America. It has spread across the world following the introduction of vaccination programs aimed at wiping out childhood diseases. For example in Iraq, autism was unknown before the Gulf War. After the war, a childhood vaccination program was started and autistic children promptly began to appear in that country. The same thing happened in Kuwait. This experimental evidence confirms the conclusion of American independent physicians and scientists. But how could a program to benefit our children possibly have such a devastating effect?

The answer is simple: the vaccines included a substance designed to preserve them during storage and transport. This substance, called thimerosol, was discovered about 1930 by scientists at Eli Lilley pharmaceuticals and proved to be a remarkably effective sterilant. Physicians investigating its usefulness soon found that it was also dangerous. The active ingredient in thimerosol is mercury which has a long history of use by the medical profession. It also has a reputation for damaging patients.

When tested in 1977, a 1% topical ointment used as a treatment for umbilical cord infections killed 10 out of 13 children. Those who died had very little mercury in their hair and fingernails. Those who lived had lots of mercury in their hair and fingernails. Evidently, infants whose bodies couldn't excrete mercury fast enough died of mercury poisoning. The physicians in charge of that test recommended that thimerosol be kept out of hospitals because it was too dangerous!

In Haley's laboratory experiments, testosterone potentiated the toxicity of mercury and estrogen suppressed it. Haley said he believes this is why boys are affected so much more than girls.

He reported that amounts injected into the blood stream of infants before their blood-brain barrier was fully developed were 50-100 times as high as the Environmental Protection Agency says is a safe level for mercury ingested through the mouth.

Laboratory studies show that tubulin, a component of neurons essential for their proper functioning in the brain, is denatured by thimerosol. Thimerosol disappears quickly after injection because it dissociates in the presence of water and salts in the body to form ethyl mercury, a far more toxic substance than elemental mercury. Vaccines also contain aluminum, which synergistically makes mercury even more toxic. The presence of lead also increases the toxicity of mercury and lead is still being leached from old pipes in many urban locations. Antibiotics also potentiate mercury.

Haley believes that the United States has experienced an unprecedented disaster as a result of a general mercurial toxemia, which is being ignored by medical authorities. He has been concerned about it and has attempted many times over the past 15 years, without success, to get the FDA and the vaccine branch of the CDC to recognize this problem.

Possibly as a response to such efforts (although not officially acknowledged), the decision to remove thimerosal from pediatric vaccines in the United States was made in 1999. The American Academy of Pediatrics claims that all routinely recommended infant vaccines are now free of the preservative. However, Drs. Mark and David Geier revealed that the 2003 Physicians' Desk Reference reported that Merck's pediatric hepatitis B vaccine contained 12.5 mcg of thimerosal per dose and the adult version contained 25 mcg per dose. Wyeth and Aventis Pasteur vaccines also contained this preservative. All influenza vaccines contain it, and they are being recommended for children.

Package inserts are labeled per FDA regulations, and it is a criminal offense to mislabel products. Yet a spokesman for Aventis Pasteur told Geiers that the company had ceased selling DtaP, a pediatric vaccine, in the preservative formulation in March 2001 and that their 2003 version's package insert, which listed thimerosal, was incorrect.

180

The World Health Organization believes that the complete removal of thimerosal from vaccines is unlikely because it is needed to kill bacteria during the nonsterile manufacturing process. It may also be an integral part of that process and thus may not serve primarily as a preservative. Consequently "preservative free" vaccines may not be free of thimerosal.

The Children's Health Act of 2000 established an Interagency Autism Coordinating Committee with a 10-year goal of preventing 25% of autism cases through early intervention and the development of better ways to treat it. Complete prevention, however, does not seem to be an objective. The medical establishment and their congressional allies continue to turn a blind eye to the likeliest causes of autism and related diseases, but that is hardly surprising when one considers the issue of legal and financial liability. Imagine the lawsuits that would follow in the wake of any admission that mercury and/or mercury compounds were directly related to the occurrence of autism and autism related disorders.

The November 2004 University of California (Berkeley) *Wellness Letter* advised its readers that all is well in Vaccine land. Thimerosol does not release mercury in the body; people are unnecessarily concerned. Is this simply evidence that Haley is right when he suggests that many good doctors are dumb chemists?

Thimerisol is not the only source of mercury affecting children. Mercury from amalgam fillings in a mother's teeth is transferred to infants during gestation. The more fillings the greater the transfer. Women with more than 10 amalgam fillings and a high concentration of testosterone in their amniotic fluid are likely to have an autistic child.

Amalgam fillings were introduced into dental practice in this country around 1860. By about 1880, a uniquely American disease called neurasthenia, or "American nervousness," appeared. Interestingly enough, relief of severe neurological conditions by removal of amalgam fillings was reported over 100 years ago in this country and 75 years ago in Germany.

The World Health Organization has reported that mercury amalgams are the major contributor to human body burdens of mercury. The Environmental Protection Agency and the National Academy of Sciences reported that 8 to 10% of American women have so much mercury in their bodies that any child they produce will have an elevated risk for neurodevelopmental problems. Additionally, 85% of dentists and dental technicians tested were found to have mercury related toxicities, and 15% were found to have mercury induced neurological deficits. These facts indicate that mercury in amalgam fillings represents a serious health risk for both ourselves and our children. This problem should also concern our national defense establishment. Our children are their future soldiers, sailors, airmen, and marines!

For a great many years dentists and the American Dental Association have maintained that their silver fillings do no harm. In August 2006, the *FDA's Update Review of Potential Adverse Health Risks Associated with Exposure to Mercury in Dental Amalgams* was published by the National Center for Toxicological Research. It asserted that dental amalgams were not a problem. The American Dental Association continued promoting their use and the Alzheimer's Association of America supported them. In spite of official assertions, however, the laws of chemistry and physics are not subject to congressional lobbying or political pressure, and mercury vapor is detectable in the mouths of people with amalgam fillings after they drink a cup of hot coffee.

In July 2009, the FDA issued its Final Regulation on Dental Amalgams. In essence, it reclassified them from I – low risk, to II - Moderate Risk. It was like pulling teeth to achieve a change in their 2006 position, published in their *Update Review of Potential Adverse Health Risks*, that dental amalgams were low risk devices. It took a class-action lawsuit filed by consumer advocate groups and some dentists to accomplish this feat. Nevertheless, the American Dental Association still maintains that amalgam "is a safe, affordable, and durable material that has been used in the teeth of more than 100 million Americans." Since the FDA didn't restrict the use of amalgam, they expect little to change in dental offices. Dr. Jerry Simon, a Connecticut dentist, believes that their fear of possible law suits is the reason they refuse to admit mercury is dangerous.

Dr. Haley believes that manufacturers of amalgam products should be required to provide in their packages data describing the amount of mercury vapor that escapes daily from an amalgam of known weight and surface area under conditions that mimic the mouth with respect to temperature, acidity, and brushing. He thinks that, if they did, it would become clear that amalgams were dangerous to health.

It is not always easy to determine if you have a toxic burden of mercury in your body. The simple 24-hour urine test that most physicians depend on is not reliable. Unlike many toxins, mercury buries itself in your cells. Your cells need help, in the form of glutathione, to get it out again. Experts use a mercury challenge test, which requires a strong chelating compound to dislodge this element from your cells, in addition to a urine test. Only about 8% of the mercury that leaves your body passes through your kidneys. The rest is processed through your liver and winds up in stool.

MERCURY AND HEART DISEASE

Idiopathic dilated cardiomyopathy, which has claimed the lives of a number of athletes who dropped dead for no apparent reason, and which caused a number of older people to require heart transplants, also has a mercury connection. German investigators found high concentrations of mercury in damaged hearts — 22,000 times the usual level of mercury in heart muscle. The cardiovascular systems of autistic infants are also adversely affected by mercury.

After I acquired chronic mercurial toxicity by breathing air containing the vapor from mercury on the floor of a university laboratory I was no longer able to swim long distances. I was told by my family physician that mercury toxicity had adversely affected part of my heart's electrical controls system - the atrioventricular bundle. But medical experts at the university maintained that I did not have mercury poisoning. They were good at avoiding responsibility - just as medical experts today are refusing to admit that mercury is damaging our children.

MERCURY AND ALZHEIMER'S DISEASE

At a meeting of Doctors for Disaster

Preparedness, Dr. Boyd Haley stated that: "mercury, and only mercury, produced the plaque and tangles characteristic of Alzheimer's disease." His research group and the Alzheimer's disease group at Kentucky University found mercury in the brains of deceased Alzheimer patients. They also found that the fingernails of these patients contained diminishing amounts of mercury as the disease progressed.

When they reported these findings their funds were cut off and their research project was turned over to a Dr. Stanley R. Saxe, professor of periodontics and geriatric dentistry at the University of Kentucky, who proceeded to find that there was no connection between the mercury in amalgam fillings and Alzheimer's disease. His report was published in a dental magazine probably because more scientifically oriented publications refused to accept it.

There is reason to believe that the risk of Alzheimer's disease is related to exposure to mercury. For example, flu vaccines contain 250,000 nanomoles of mercury per shot. There is evidence that adults who receive one of these each year for 5 years have a substantially increased risk of developing the disease. Deplorably, these same flu vaccines, containing twice as much mercury as pediatric vaccines used to have, are now recommended for children. It is very disturbing that a substance that *killed* children, when applied as a topical ointment, is being injected directly into their bloodstreams.

SOURCES OF MERCURY

Years ago mercury was used as a depilatory to remove hair from animal skins in the hat industry.

Many workers in this industry acquired mental diseases on the job - hence the "Mad Hatter" in <u>Alice in Wonderland</u>. Although mercury thermometers are no longer used to measure patients' temperatures in hospitals or to monitor conditions in laboratories, mercury is still ubiquitous. It is present in the "energy-saving" fluorescent light bulbs, in many thermostats, and even in some light switches. Exposure to mercury, like exposure to radiation, is practically unavoidable.

Mercury is in the fish we eat and in the air we breathe. Most air-borne mercury reaches us from Asian and African sources. Coal fired power plants in China produce lots of it and air currents carry it across the Pacific Ocean. Miners in Brazil use mercury in gold recovery processes and much of it ultimately winds up in the ocean. American coal fired power plants add relatively small amounts, perhaps 3%, of the total in air, since environmental regulations require most of it to be removed from stack gases before they are allowed to enter the atmosphere. There are natural sources as well, such as volcanoes.

Our bodies are naturally equipped to eliminate small amounts of toxins, including mercury. Most of the capability (about two thirds) is in our digestive systems. Therefore, ingested mercury, like that found in fish and other foods, is not as great a threat as that which enters our bodies in other ways, like breathing, absorption through the skin and membranes, or direct injection into the bloodstream.

If it is impossible to remove mercury from vaccines entirely because of the way in which these products are manufactured, is there an alternative way of dealing with childhood diseases? Fortunately, the answer is YES! About 70 years ago Dr. Frederick Klenner cured childhood diseases with vitamin C injections. But medical schools do not teach students how to use Klenner's technology, and physicians can lose their licenses to practice medicine if they dare to use it. For more about Klenner see the Chapter on Infectious Diseases.

CHAPTER 8 - RADIATION

It will come as a surprise to many that we need ionizing radiation to keep us healthy just as we need food, water, and air. The average American is very much underexposed with only 300 millirem per year of background radiation. T. D. Luckey, ScD, former Chairman of the Biochemistry Department of the University of Missouri, has said that we need much more than 10 times as much for optimal health. Healthy people have been living in Ramsari, Iran, where radiation levels average 48,000 mr/yr, for over 2,000 years. Furthermore, we cannot escape radiation because we are all emitting ionizing radiation and we may be energized by it. Dr. Luckey estimates that the average person experiences roughly 1 radioactive emission in every cell of his /her body every hour from internal sources.

A great many people in America have been conned into fear of any kind of radiation. There is no doubt that too much ionizing radiation can do great damage, but too little of it can damage us, too. Our bodies were designed to function in a much more radioactive environment than exists today. Furthermore, low levels of whole body radiation have been shown to be capable of curing cancer in both this country and Japan.

RESIDENTIAL RADON LEVELS AND LUNG CANCER

After completing the most intensive and expensive ecological study ever made, Dr. Bernard Cohen, a liberal Democrat, Professor Emeritus of the University of Pittsburg, and a respected physicist, shut off the $1,200 radon reduction system in his home to save electricity. He had proven, beyond the shadow of a doubt, that increasing amounts of radiation from radon were associated with decreasing lung cancer death rates in the United States.

To be specific, Cohen found that death rates from this disease decreased from about 72 per year per 10,000 men when exposure to radon was close to zero picocuries per liter, to about 42 per year per 10,000 men when exposure was about 6 picocuries per liter. He spent a lot of time attempting to make the data he had collected from homes in 1,729 counties, a sampling of 90% of the United States, fit the Linear No Threshold (LNT) theory, which provides the basis for our "Radon Laws." The objective of his study was to validate the theory, but no matter what sophisticated correction he attempted, the data refused to support the theory. It should be noted that this theory had been controversial from the time it was promulgated by the National Academy of Sciences.

Fear of radiation has been promoted via an unverified assumption that has been proven to be

189

incorrect by exhaustive investigation in the United States. The health effect of high levels of radiation, in terms of cancer rates versus exposure were well documented after World War II. The result was a chart which showed a linear correlation between the incidence of cancer and exposure to ionizing radiation over a wide range of exposures. Unfortunately, substantially no data was available for very low rates of exposure. The National Academy of Sciences formed a committee to decide what to do about this deficiency. After much discussion, Dr. Linus Pauling proposed the assumption that no effect should be expected from the absence of radiation and that, therefore, it was reasonable to extend the existing linear relationship between radiation exposure and cancer rates to zero. In effect this meant that no level of ionizing radiation was safe! Some scientists at that meeting are reported to have objected to Pauling's hypothesis, but it was adopted. Later research disproved it. [24]

With the cachet of the National Academy of Sciences, the LNT theory became establishment doctrine. Political activists, especially those intent on limiting use of nuclear energy, had a field day. They used the theory to generate the current "Radon Laws" and also to discourage the construction of new nuclear power facilities. It would seem that they are still powerful.

---

24 Bernard Cohen's extensive investigation of the effects of radon on lung cancer, much later, was definitive.

Despite the inability of a multi-year, multi-million dollar study to prove the LNT theory, the National Academy of Sciences, once again, on June 29, 2005, reaffirmed its position. It is still political dogma that there is no lower limit to the cancer causing effects of ionizing radiation.

Meanwhile, Americans are still paying for electricity to remove from their basements a gas whose radiation could help protect them against cancer. The dead hand of the law still maintains the defunct theory and supports another monopoly to protect Americans from a non-existent threat. This is a case of politically modified science. The suppression of science is a profitable, multifaceted business.

IONIZING RADIATION CAN BE USEFUL

A newly published book by Ed Hiserodt, Underexposed, contains a startling piece of information that needs to be added to everybody's store: Children growing up in areas supposedly damaged by the Chernobyl nuclear disaster are super kids!!!

They are growing faster, have higher IQ's, and better immune systems than comparable children!! Professor Vladimir Mikhalev of Bryansk State University has been following their progress since 1986 and claims that they are tops in tests! Paul Harvey is said to have disclosed these interesting facts to his radio audience, but otherwise it has been a well-kept secret.

According to the International Atomic Energy Agency, between 100,000 and 200,000 European babies were aborted by their mothers, after the Chernobyl disaster because they thought they might give birth to monsters. What has the world lost because of misinformation and hysteria?

It is time to become acquainted with facts about ionizing radiation and to realize that environmental activists have saddled us with a lot of expensive and unnecessary boondoggles which contribute to expense, pain, and suffering rather than protect us from danger.

Early evidence that ionizing radiation might be beneficial was obtained in 1943 during the Manhattan Project when rats were raised in an atmosphere heavily contaminated with uranium dust in an effort to establish its toxicity. These lucky rats lived longer and reproduced at a higher rate than the uncontaminated controls. Additional evidence of the beneficial effects of low levels of radiation was obtained during studies of the survivors of the Hiroshima and Nagasaki bombings, but was rejected because the few data points were inconsistent with the LNT theory. It is now a well-established fact that atom bomb survivors, who were exposed to low levels of radiation, are living longer with less disease than those who were not exposed.

In l980, Professor T.D. Luckey, former Chairman of the Biochemistry Department of the University of Missouri School of Medicine published a book Hormesis with Ionizing Radiation, which contains a great deal of information on the effects of small amounts of radiation on non-mammals. In 1991, he published <u>Radiation Hormesis</u> on the beneficial effects of hormetic radiation on man and other mammals. His data indicate that the optimum dose is about 10,000 millirems (mrem) per year.

The following table, extracted from Hiserodt's book, indicates that this optimum amount of radiation is not easily available. It explains why an acquaintance in Oregon said that he would like to obtain some spent fuel to make cement blocks to put around his foundation. In his opinion, the background radiation level in Oregon is much too low.

	millirem per yr
EPA proposed maximum	100
U.S. Average Background	300
Chernobyl Area	500
Colorado Plateau	600
Kerala India	1,300
Gerais, Brazil	2,300
Guarapari Beach, Brazil	26,300
Ramsari, Iran (average)	48,000

Note that people have been living in Ramsari for at least 2,000 years.

While our savants at the National Academy of Sciences and the EPA are warning us to be very, very careful of tiny amounts of that bad ionizing radiation, the French National Academy of Sciences and the National Academy of Medicine take a different position in a May 2005 unanimous report: "this report doubts the validity of using LNT in the evaluation of the carcinogenic risk of low doses (<100mSv) and even more for very low doses (<10mSv).......the use of LNT in the low dose range is not consistent with radiobiological knowledge."

Convincing evidence of the beneficial effects of low dose radiation was presented in a paper published in the *Journal of American Physicians and Surgeons* in 2004, *Is Chronic Radiation a Prophylaxis against Cancer?* by W.L. Chen et. al. They revealed that exposure to Cobalt-60 with a half life of 5.3 years can be good for you. Housed for 20 years in 180 apartment buildings constructed with steel containing Cobalt-60, 10,000 lucky Taiwanese tenants experienced 3.5 cancer deaths for 100,000 person years as opposed to 116 deaths per 100,000 person years in the general population. A 97% reduction in cancer rates was free. There was no increase in their rents.

TOXIC WASTE OR TOXIC DECISIONS?

It is interesting to know that our government plans to spend about $1,000 per US family cleaning up the radioactive Hanford waste site. The excessive exposure being removed is less than people used to get during shoe fittings years ago – about 175 mrem/yr. Present plans are to pour almost $1 trillion dollars down rat holes like this.

During the Carter Administration, our unwise leaders decided not to recover usable fissionable material from spent fuel but junk it. They preferred to create another bottomless pit for money, Yucca Flats, rather than recovering and using what amounts to about 95% of the expensively refined fuel originally fed to the reactors.

At the end of World War II, the United States was rich. Now it is poor. Each of our families owes the Chinese over $6,000, courtesy of the Federal Government. We can no longer afford these boondoggles. It is time for us to wake up and recognize that we have some serious problems and look for economical solutions.

One of our most important problems is a supply of low cost energy. Unjustified fear of radiation has prevented us from constructing nuclear power plants for 30 years. The practical French obtain over 75% of their energy requirements from such plants. The Chinese have taken the lead in pebble bed reactor design and plan, not only to use lots of them themselves, but sell them around the world. India is building a 500 megawatt breeder reactor and planning to build four more. Even Iran and Brazil plan to generate energy by splitting atoms. The Russians will no longer send their radioactive waste to us because they also intend to build a breeder reactor.

With present day knowledge, we could build breeder reactors which could even burn thorium, readily available almost everywhere. According to Dr.

Teller, now deceased, these reactors could supply us with ample supplies of energy for the next 100,000 years. What is holding us back? If it is fear of another Chernobyl, let's look at the facts.

EFFECTS OF RADIATION IN THE CHERNOBYL EXCLUSION ZONE

The November-December 2005 issue of the *American Scientist*, published by Sigma Xi, the Scientific Research Society, provides evidence that radiation exposure is not as lethal as anti-nuclear activists would have us believe. After 12 years of research on animals in the Chernobyl exclusion zone, Professors Ronald K. Chesser and Robert J. Baker, both associated with Texas Tech University, have found no evidence of increased mutation rates among either the indigenous rodents or those imported into this radioactive area as controls. In fact, they concluded that mice have a natural "immunity" to harm from radiation. They also mention that a previous article of theirs, published in *Nature* in April 1996, that reported an elevated rate of genetic mutations among voles in the exclusion zone, had been withdrawn. Analysis of their samples with more accurate instrumentation invalidated their former conclusion.

Experiments with transgenic mice, which carry a gene that glows "blue" if it mutates, and with radiosensitive mice, indicated that genetic impacts of exposure to levels of radiation in the exclusion zone are subtle. They are unlikely to threaten reproductive success or longevity. The professors found no evidence of increased mutation rates from exposure to radiation. Mice in this area were found to have radioactive cesium in their muscles and radioactive strontium in their bones because these are the predominant radio nuclides remaining in the area. They were radioactive mice. But, since we all contain radioactive potassium and are radioactive as well, this isn't a surprise. It may have surprised the professors that the mice were so healthy, but it would not have surprised Dr. T. D. Luckey who has assembled convincing evidence that most of us are suffering from radiation deprivation and recorded it in his book Radiation Hormesis.

The exclusion zone has become a nature preserve inhabited by a wide variety of animals, large and small, with a scattering of former human inhabitants who have made their way back to their homes. The radioactive fallout initially decimated the animals, and killed pine trees, but birches survived. Now animals and trees are thriving and, according to a recent article in *National Geographic* magazine, Government services are starting to move back also. After 20 years levels of radioactivity have fallen substantially. Only 3% of the initial radioactivity remains. It may be a healthier place to live than Saranac Lake, New York, even in the area of investigation about two miles from the disaster site, where the investigators' Geiger counters were "perpetually abuzz!"

On the 20th Anniversary of the disaster, news media published estimates of the numbers of people who died as a result of the accident. The estimates ranged from over 90,000 people to the 31 identified casualties. The authors note that no one explained the reason for the differences and there is still no accurate account of deaths or of birth defects caused by the disaster. Many scientists believe that the method used to estimate these "excess deaths" is flawed. Ed Hiserodt in his book Under Exposed, claims that, excluding Hiroshima and Nagasaki, actual identified deaths from radioactive exposure, including 5 members of the general public, total 58. He says that, statistically, death from exposure to radiation in a population of 4 billion people is about as likely as death from the bite of a rabid cow.

Hiserodt's book explains how to calculate what are called "excess deaths," the dead people who remain undiscovered after radiation emissions like the Chernobyl disaster. First, you have to accept the Linear No-Threshold (LNT) Theory which assumes that there is no safe level of radiation – any amount of it will cause cancer. Then you take the total emissions whose effect is to be estimated, the "Collective Dose," and divide it by the amount of ionizing radiation equivalent to 1 excess death. For example, the Health Physics and Radiological Health Handbook states that the Global Collective Dose of Carbon -14 released by the Nuclear Power industry is 18,000 person-sieverts and 4,000 person-sieverts causes one excess death. Dividing

18,000 by 4,000 = 4.5 calculated excess deaths per year caused by the release of carbon-14 from 440 reactors.

A similar kind of calculation can be made using aspirin. "If 100 aspirins are a fatal dose for an individual, then when 100 people take 1 aspirin each, they have had a "collective dose" of 100 aspirins; therefore one of them is going to die."

Zbigniew Jaworoski, former chairman of the United Nations Committee on the Effects of Atomic Radiation, estimated that "enforcing the radiation safety regulations in the United States costs about $3 billion for each life saved by accidental exposure." We are no longer a rich country. Can we afford to continue to waste money on this scale?

More importantly, how long are we going to allow anti-nuclear activists to use this flawed, politically modified "science," to prevent us from exploiting our nuclear know-how acquired at heavy taxpayer expense? These activists are standing in the way of our access to cheap energy that doesn't require us to depend on imported oil and gas.

The issue of access to cheap energy is important. Voters should consider asking candidates what they intend to do to help us catch up with India, which is building a breeder reactor and plans to build more, and China, which has a major nuclear power building plan underway.

There is much more thorium than uranium available to us, and Edward Teller long ago suggested that using thorium fuel and breeder reactors could give us cheap energy for 100,000 years. Breeder reactors can also burn plutonium and, in this way, keep it out of the hands of potential terrorists!

SURVIVING AN ATOMIC BOMB ATTACK

Many Americans believe that, if caught in the vicinity of an atomic bomb detonation, either the initial blast, the following heat wave, and/or the radiation will kill them, or the subsequent fallout will do them in more slowly. Dr. Melvin A Bernarde's book, <u>Our Precarious Habitat</u>, published in 1970, provides convincing evidence that you will die if you are in close proximity to such a blast but equally convincing evidence that the fallout is not so lethal.

On March 1, 1954, a thermonuclear device was detonated on a barge in the Marshall Islands. Natives living on the nearby islands of Rongelap, Utirik and Alinginae, 28 airmen at a weather station on Rongerlap 160 miles away from Bikini Atoll, the site of the detonation, and 28 Japanese on the fishing vessel Fukuru Maru, were exposed to the extensive fallout. At the time, newspapers gave more than full coverage to what appeared to be an inadvertent tragedy. Fortunately, there is another side to this story.

Although the fallout was visible and extensive, the sixty-four natives of the Marshall Islands, and the twenty-three Japanese on the Lucky Dragon took no precautions to avoid it. The fishermen described the fallout as heavy as snow. It came in direct contact with their skin and eyes. It contaminated their food and water as they lived with it for 13 days until they arrived at their home port. More than two days after the incident, chemical analysis of urine indicated that the natives had received a whole body dose of 175 rem.

A few days after the detonation the natives were taken to a military hospital on Kwajalein. The fishermen were hospitalized thirteen days after the detonation when they reached port. Both the natives and the Japanese suffered skin ulcerations and hair loss. The damage to both groups was directly related to the amount of gamma radiation they received and inversely related to the amount of their skin covered by clothing during exposure. The fishermen who did not wear hats were the most severely burned.

Six months after the incident, one of the fishermen died of a diseased liver. The amount of radionuclides in his tissues was so low that radiation could not have been a factor in his death. In 1960, the islanders, who had returned to their still heavily radioactive islands 3 1/2 years after the event, were again physically examined. Both those who had been exposed to the fallout and those who hadn't were in good shape. In 1966, the appearance of thyroid nodules due to radiation damage in five natives from Rongelap resulted in their examination at the New England Deaconess Hospital in Boston. Physicians removed the nodules which were found to be non-cancerous.

It is reasonable to conclude from this information that inhalation and ingestion of radioactive fallout is not a big deal. Burns from fallout can be minimized or avoided by suitable clothing, washing exposed parts quickly and by remaining under cover for a suitable time.

In 1979, Cresson H. Kearny, now deceased, wrote a self help instruction manual for Americans interested in surviving a nuclear attack. It was published by Oak Ridge National Laboratory, a facility of the Department of Energy. It was updated by the author to include information about RADIATION HORMESIS. In oversimplified terms, it says that large quantities of radiation during a short period of time can kill you, but small quantities for long periods of time can help you. This book has been republished as a public service by the Oregon Institute of Science and Medicine in Cave Junction, Oregon, and is available over the internet. The title of the book: Nuclear War Survival Skills.

In 1945, the Atomic Bomb Casualty Commission was established to investigate the effects of the Hiroshima and Nagasaki bombings. They determined that the survivors of the bombing had received doses between 100 and 175 rads. A monumental study involving 100,000 survivors failed to show that their exposure had resulted in genetic damage to them or to their offspring. In 1970, scientists were still puzzled by these findings.

Ed Hiserodt's book, Underexposed, published in 2005, contains additional information about these survivors. They are living longer than the unexposed, they are in better health, and their children are not monsters. So are the survivors of the Russian reactor disaster at Chernobyl. The reason, as Hiserodt suggests, is that our bodies are built to operate in an environment which is far more radioactive than our present one. Too little radiation adversely affects our immune and DNA repair systems. Experts believe that the optimum exposure to background radiation is about 10,000 millirem per year, orders of magnitude more than the average exposure of 300 millirem per year in the United States.

Unfortunately, it is difficult to interest official America in the possibility of ordinary people surviving a nuclear attack. The possibility of mutual destruction is deemed sufficient to prevent nuclear war. This policy decision eliminates the need to protect the public. It is only necessary to make sure that Federal Government officials survive and millions have been spent providing facilities for their protection not too far away from Washington, D. C.

Research by members of Doctors for Disaster Preparedness has revealed that the Swiss, the Russians, and the Chinese are well equipped with the means to protect their own people. The Swiss are said to have more space in their shelter system than there are people in that country. Chairman Mao once said that he was not concerned about nuclear war because he was sure some Chinese would survive. The Chinese are reported to have an extensive system of underground shelters. The Russians claim that, because their fallout shelters do not have indigenous water supplies, they aren't fallout shelters.

A new $10 device that can reduce vulnerability to nuclear attack is now available. The **Self-indicating Instant Radiation Alert Dosimeter** (SIRAD), developed by Gordon Patel with government money, is approved by the Department of Homeland Security. It joins the Kearny fallout meter, and the NukAlert, as devices available to Americans who want to enhance their chances of surviving nearby nuclear explosions. Geiger counters, which used to be available for first responders, were ordered to be turned in and disposed of by the Clinton administration. Arizona is the only state in which all first responders are prepared for nuclear attacks. The probability of such attacks has been increasing. A postage stamp size SIRAD can be made to sell for $2, cheap enough for general use.

If you are interested in surviving a nuclear attack, don't expect any help from Washington. There is no plan for the survival of mere mortals. You will have to take care of yourself. Cresson Kearney's contribution to your survival is your best bet, in my opinion.

RADIATION FROM THE EARTH

According to Dr. Luckey, ScD, the earth has been about 10 times more radioactive in the past than it is now, although there hasn't been much change since humans appeared four million years ago. His book,

<u>Radiation Hormesis,</u> states that most of earth's radioactivity is generated by three long-lived radioactive families of elements headed by the uraniums: U235 and U238, and thorium Th232. Once there was a lot of U235, the highly radioactive uranium isotope used in atomic bombs and nuclear reactors, now only very small amounts of it remain. Early on it, and its progeny, were the main sources of heat and radioactivity. Now the families of U238 and Th232 perform this function.

The top foot of a square kilometer of average soil, which contains about 1,000 kilograms (Kg) of uranium, 2,000 Kg of thorium and 0.4 grams (gms) of radium releases 1.5 mGy of radon into the air each year.

A few other elements, such as potassium, rubidium, and samarium, have radioactive isotopes. Most have little impact on living things. Potassium is an exception. Its radioactive isotope, K40, with a half life of 1.3 billion years, has a big impact.

INTERNAL SOURCES

Non-radioactive sodium plays an important role outside our cells, but radioactive and non-radioactive potassium are inside every one of them. K40 is 0.0118% of the potassium which has an important physiological role inside our cells. Each of us has inside our bodies about 17 milligrams. They produce about 0.17 millisieverts per year (mSv/yr, 1 sievert = 100 millirem) of absorbed radiation, most of it inside our cells.

Radioactive potassium has a short biological half life of 16 days, but is continually replaced by the food we eat. Each 100 disintegrations results in 11 gamma rays, 89 beta rays, and 23 delta rays. The relatively low-energy delta waves may energize the mitochondria, the power plants in our cells, which generate the adenosine triphosphate (ATP) which keeps our bodies functioning. The conversion of sugar into carbon dioxide and water supplies the energy needed to form the triphosphate from adenosine diphosphate. Conceivably the disintegration of potassium produces the energy to deconstruct sugar. In any case, disintegrations in the water environment inside cells produce highly active free radicals like hydroxyl ions and electrons.

Uranium, thorium, and actinium inside our bodies, mainly in our bones, add to our radioactive load of about 0.4 mSv/yr. Sleeping with your spouse exposes you to about 0.04 milligrays per year (mGy/yr, 1 gray = 100 rads of incident radiation). Associating with co-workers adds perhaps 0.02 mSv/yr additional absorbed radiation. Practically everything radiates all the time, including buildings, and even the granite countertops in many kitchens.

COSMIC RADIATION

Each year, we get about 0.4 mGy/yr from cosmic radiation. It has been estimated that, if we live about 1,000 feet above sea level, each of our cells is hit once a day by a cosmic ray. Mountaineers at 3,000 meters receive 1 mGy/yr, 3 times the radiation of people living at sea level. Crews of commercial aircraft may get about 1.5mGy/yr from cosmic rays.

MEDICAL SOURCES

Medical diagnostic procedures provide us with about 0.54 mGy/yr, 0.4 from X-rays, and 0.14 from radiopharmaceuticals. Physicians and radiation technicians are often ignorant about radiation, according to Dr. Luckey. Nurses and radiation technicians may absorb one mGy/yr. Patients leaving hospitals frequently emit high levels of radiation by public health standards but low levels by medical risk standards. A patient may discharge more radioactivity than allowable by a nuclear power plant, Luckey believes that unpublicized medical accidents have caused injuries and deaths through use of obsolete equipment, omission of filters, insufficient distance from sources, incorrect X-ray machine settings, and overdoses to surface structures during deep therapy.

RADIATION FROM OUR FOOD

Average exposure of adults in the United States from their food and drink is estimated to be 0.03 mGy/yr. Measurable amounts of strontium 89, strontium 90, cesium 137, and radium 226, besides K40 are found in our foods. Nuts, meat and seafood have the highest concentrations, in that order. Food sterilized with either electron beams or Co60 did not adversely affect four generations of mice and does not become more radioactive by reason of the irradiation. Foods in Kerala, India, where healthy people have been living for 2,000 years, may contain as much as three times the radioactivity of similar foods in the United States.

WHY WE NEED RADIATION

Low doses of ionizing radiation stimulate physiological functions in our bodies, but high doses are destructive. There is a parallel in the field of medicine. Practically all medications are poisons in large doses, although they may have very beneficial effects in low doses. In nutrition, selenium was once considered poisonous and carcinogenic. In small amounts it is now known to be an essential nutriment and anti- tumor agent. The word used to describe this condition is hormesis. The practice of Homeopathy, an alternative to Allopathic Medicine, is based on hormesis.

A considerable amount of experimental evidence exists that exposure to low doses of whole body radiation stimulates the immune and DNA repair systems in our bodies. A more competent immune system decreases the effects of infections and cancer and leads to less disease and longer life. An activated DNA repair system permits, not only faster recovery from damage, but also temporary protection from higher doses of radiation than those which caused the activation. The children of healthy men exposed to energizing doses of whole body radiation have been found to live longer than average, but, it should be noted that radiation concentrated in a small area is destructive. Dentists, years ago lost fingers which they used to hold X-ray plates inside patients' mouths. Physicians use radiation to destroy cancerous tissue, usually with collateral damage to healthy tissue.

Over 90% of radiation effects begin with the formation of free radicals. Since water represents about 80% of soft tissue and 99.9% of the molecules inside cells, most of the free radicals are fragments of water molecules. The OH, hydroxyl radical, appears to be the most reactive species. Cascades of free radical reactions can form stable compounds capable of affecting cells throughout the body. These hydroxyl radicals, therefore, appear to be what causes the hormesis effect at low levels of whole body ionizing radiation as well as extensive damage at high levels.

Dr. Luckey maintains that the optimum level of radiation for us humans is 100 mGy/yr. He also believes that we need ionizing radiation in order to survive. It is an essential component of our nutrition, like vitamins. Most of us are exposed to far too little radiation and would benefit greatly from more exposure.

Luckey backs up his conclusions with reams of data from years of scientific investigations. Those who have sold us the idea that all radiation is dangerous and should be avoided have an assumption underlying their hype and hysteria – but no convincing DATA!! Let the truth be known!!!

CHAPTER 9 - NUTRITION

While a majority of Americans are convinced of the importance of nutrition in health care, and buy and use, dietary supplements and want to continue to do so, the FDA and other members of the medical monopoly downplay their importance and discourage their use. Efforts to turn supplements into drugs, available only by prescription, resulted in such public outrage that Congress was impelled to pass the Dietary Supplement Health and Education Act (DHSEA). This was signed into law by President Clinton in 1994 to protect the right of Americans to have access to therapeutic amounts of supplements. Nevertheless, the fight for control of supplements continues.

Drug companies are attempting to gain control of the competition by acquiring supplement suppliers and their allies in the FDA are continuing to push for limits on the number of dietary supplements that can be sold to the public and the amounts that can be purchased without a physician's prescription. A new weapon against American free choice and the protection of the DSHEA is the UN sponsored Codex Alimentarious [25].

---

25 (Latin for "food book") It is a collection of internationally recognized standards, codes of practice, guidelines and other recommendations relating to foods, food production and food safety.

A <u>Codex</u> Alimentations, or food code, began functioning in 1893 in the Austro-Hungarian Empire. It provided guideline for courts in cases dealing with food. It went out of existence in 1918 after the breakup of the empire. In 1962, the United Nations decided a new <u>Codex</u> should be implemented to protect the health of the consumers of the world. The effort is funded by the Food and Agriculture Organization and the World Health Organization. In 2002, both organizations became concerned about its direction and hired a consultant to evaluate its performance and recommend action. The consultant is said to have recommended its elimination. However, it is alleged that industrial interests, recognizing an opportunity for profit, influenced a change in the consultant's report. It was revised to suggest that the <u>Codex</u> address twenty concerns within the organization.

Since 2002, American consumer activists have managed, with difficulty, to observe the <u>Codex</u> committee in action and to make their views known to the Committee during its sessions. They are particularly concerned because the Committee, under German leadership, as Germany is the host country, has already been able to prevent access to many food supplements in several European countries, Australia, Canada, and Great Britain. Since the United States is a member of the World Trade Organization, it too can be required to accept <u>Codex</u> rulings under threat of expensive trade sanctions. At these meetings it is reported that American representatives from the Food and Drug

Administration are not objecting to the restrictions being placed on consumers. According to Dr. Gregory Damato, one of the American consumer activists following Codex activities, the United States government supports the Codex agenda and one of its representatives became chairman of the Committee at a recent meeting.

Damato says that some Codex standards were to take effect on December 31, 2009, and that FDA policy, adopted in 1995, states that international standards (Codex) supersede US laws governing food. Furthermore he claims that the 2004 Central American Free Trade Agreement required us to conform to Codex in December 2009. It is well known that membership in the World Trade Organization requires us to adopt Codex and it has the means to apply pressure via expensive trade sanctions.

Our FDA, which is taking a leading role in Codex affairs, has expressed some interesting opinions in a recent legal brief involving the transport of privately owned unpasteurized milk according to Doreen Hanna at www.NewsWithViews.com.

> "There is no right to consume or feed children any particular food."

> "There is no generalized right to bodily and physical health."

213

The FDA argues that Plaintiffs' assertion of a "fundamental right to their own bodily and physical health, which includes what foods they do and do not choose to consume for themselves and their families" is unavailing because plaintiffs do not have a fundamental right to obtain any food they wish.

A major objective of <u>Codex</u> appears to be to block consumer access to therapeutic quantities of vitamins, minerals, and other food supplements. It will also limit the number available for sale to consumers. If it is successful here, our sickness industries will flourish, which may be why drug companies are said to be supporting the <u>Codex</u> agenda. As a by-product, life expectancies may be reduced enough to take care of the Social Security, and Medicare and Medicaid budget shortfalls which are expected to become unmanageable as 80 million baby boomers retire in the next 20 years.

Codex is a serious threat to the health and welfare of Americans, but some of our senators and congressmen seem intent on making it the law of the land. They have introduced a series of bills that, if passed, would have opened the way for <u>Codex</u>. Fortunately, consistent widespread opposition has prevented action on these bills, but that does not seem to have discouraged them.

<u>DISEASE AND YOUR DIET</u>

As mentioned previously, Hippocrates of Cos, long known as the "father of medicine", is reported to have pontificated: "Let food be your medicine and medicine be your food." In more recent times I was told: "You are what you eat." Years ago Congress was told that our soils have been depleted of minerals. Factory farms add only nitrogen, phosphorus, potassium, and sulphur to the soils. Other minerals are not advertised as fertilizers, although in Germany some farmers are known to spread certain rock dusts on their fields to increase mineralization. Depleted soils cannot be expected to produce high quality foods. Fungicides, pesticides, antibiotics, and hormones also have their effects on those who consume treated foodstuffs.

To make up for the deficiencies in our foods, supplements are required. Our bodies need a number of food supplements, in adequate quantities, to be optimally healthy, and the requirements for these essential things vary from one person to another and they also vary as the physical condition of each person varies. The needs for dietary supplements of a healthy young man on a farm in Iowa are substantially different from the needs of a sick old woman in a nursing home in New York City. Also the needs of the healthy young man increase if he gets sick despite these variations.

A Federal government directive presumes to tell us our daily requirements for a whole list of essential nutriments. These requirements are usually based on tests of healthy young men. Strict adherence to these guidelines is not in our best interests. They can prevent our enjoyment of optimal health.

An important part of our medical monopoly, the AMA, has controlled medical education for about 100 years. The vast majority of medical students graduate with inadequate training in nutrition which clearly indicates that the monopoly is not interested in this field. Nevertheless, medical authorities are not afraid to tell their patients, and sometimes the general public, what they should and should not eat. For example, after President Eisenhower's heart attack, his physician, Dr. Dudley White, told Americans to avoid meat and fat to keep their hearts healthy. When two Arctic explorers proved that he was wrong, he had the good grace to publicly admit his error.

According to Caleb Finch in The Biology of Human Longevity, our ancestors doubled their life expectancies when they started to eat meat and fat more than a million years ago. Of course these foods were obtained from wild animals not cattle, poultry and fish pumped full of antibiotics and hormones. Meat products offered for sale now are not as nutritious as they used to be. There is a reasonable probability that present day products cause problems with our glandular systems. It is hard to gage the effect of this change in our food supply on public health, but there is little doubt that it has helped increase the incidence of disease.

As Dr. Rodger J. Williams, who discovered the vitamin pantothenic acid and was the first biochemist to be elected President of the American Chemical Society, noted: "There are about 40 growth and maintenance chemicals which, along with oxygen, water and energy-producing food, make healthy life possible." Animal experiments have shown that, if any one of these is missing from the diet, animals will fail to develop properly and will die before maturity. For example when vitamin A was eliminated from the diet of high grade breeding sows their piglets were born with no eyeballs and had many other birth defects.

A human baby needs every kind of growth and maintenance chemical at the right time during its development in its mother's womb. Inadequate nutrition during pregnancy causes many tragedies. There are about 500,000 miscarriages, and 125,000 mentally retarded children born in the United States every year. The many infants with birth defects add to our national costs of health care. It is reasonable to believe that insuring the proper nutrition of pregnant women would pay big dividends. In this connection note that Dr. Klenner, mentioned in the chapter on Infectious Diseases, supervised the prenatal care of hundreds of women, none of whom had miscarriages or mentally retarded children. Their children were called vitamin C babies by the nurses who took care of them because their mothers took lots of vitamin C during pregnancy and most received a shot of it just before delivery. He also supervised the first successful delivery of quadruplets in the United States. His training in biochemistry (he had two degrees in this subject before entering medical school) gave him a proper respect for nutrition.

In contrast to Klenner's respect for nutrition, consider the effects of the AMA's disrespect. In 1955, a Vanderbilt University study by W. J. Darby and W. J. McGanity concluded that poor diet had no effect on pregnant women or their babies unless it resulted in a deficiency disease. As a result, physicians told pregnant women that they shouldn't gain more than 17 pounds, dietary supplements were needless and extravagant, standards of calorie intake were too high and to use diuretics to lose weight if necessary. The result of this advice was a generation of low birth weight babies with a high percentage of neurological disabilities. These 1960's babies were also said to be especially vulnerable to neurological damage from childhood vaccines.

In 1969, a White House conference on food, nutrition, and health concluded that the teaching of nutrition in medical, dental, and nursing schools was inadequate. In some schools it was non-existent. Nevertheless, the FDA campaigned for years, with the support of the AMA, against improving the American diet with health foods and dietary supplements.

In 1953, and again in 1958, the FDA attacked "myths" such as: disease is caused by faulty diet; over-processed foods, and sub-clinical deficiencies. In 1961, FDA Commissioner George Landry said: "The most widespread and expensive quack in the US is the promotion of vitamins and food supplements." In 1970, the FDA proclaimed that vitamins and minerals promoted as treatments or cures for disease were drugs. In 1977, the Deputy Director of the National Cancer

Institute (NCI) noted that the role of nutrition in disease was recognized only for specific syndromes like beri beri, scurvy, and rickets. About the same time an FDA news release stated that there is no solid evidence that vitamin E is good for heart disease in humans and that a deficiency was highly improbable. It also stated that there is no sound scientific basis of the need for vitamins if you have a reasonably normal diet and that the statement that all people need to supplement their diets with vitamins and minerals is nutritional quackery!

The FDA Task Force on Dietary Foods and Supplements final report in 1992 asked: "What steps are necessary to insure that the existence of dietary supplements on the market does not act as a disincentive for drug development?" It noted the strong desire of American consumers to have access to dietary supplements, which the FDA tended to ignore in the past.

OUR DAILY BREAD – IS IT AS GOOD AS IT CAN BE?

In 1959, Frank G. Boudreau, MD, formerly a member of the Food and Nutrition Board, wrote the following in the Department of Agriculture's Yearbook: "If all we know about nutrition were applied to modern society, the result would be an enormous improvement in public health, at least equal to that which resulted when the germ theory of disease was made the basis of public health and medical work."

In 1973, Rodger J. Williams noted that Dr. Boudreau was calling for a revolution in medicine. At that time Williams believed that, based on extensive evidence, such a revolution might soon occur. Unfortunately, things we knew in 1973 are still not being applied in 2010 for the benefit of the people who paid for their discovery - American taxpayers.

"Give us this day our daily bread" has been a part of the prayers of a majority of our people from the start of our American Republic. Bread has been a staple in the diet of Homo sapiens since agriculture had its beginning and made civilization possible. Is the bread available today as good as it can be? It was not in Rodger Williams' day. Currently most people believe that stone ground whole wheat bread is the best that can be. But is it? Williams thought we were aiming too low.

WHITE BREAD EQUALS MALNUTRITION?

The potential value of applications of advanced nutritional science is illustrated by Williams' 1973 publication *"Should the Science Based Food Industry be expected to Advance?"* In it, he depicts what happened to four different strains of mice fed two different kinds of bread. One was commercial white bread. The other was bread made with enriched flour fortified with a number

220

of well known dietary supplements. After 90 days, two-thirds of the mice fed the commercial white bread were dead of malnutrition and the rest were severely stunted. Most mice fed fortified bread were alive and still growing. Estimated cost of the supplements per 100 pounds of flour was 70 cents in 1973.

Williams notes that the restrictive activities of the FDA tend to hold "enrichment" at static levels. They require such large investments in tests to determine safety and effectiveness that gaining approval is only possible for wealthy corporations. Linus Pauling, PhD, believed that, since vitamins are substances to which the human body has long been accustomed, and the toxicities of water soluble vitamins are known to be low and the side effects few, it is nonsensical to subject them to as thorough testing as a new synthetic drug. In this connection it should be noted that the National Institutes of Health (NIH) is now testing sodium ascorbate, a liver metabolites, for safety. We would be making this in our own bodies if we had not lost the capability millions of years ago. Is this possibly a waste of taxpayer money?

The substances which were added to one pound of "enriched" flour in Williams experiment, in microgram or milligram amounts, are: Vitamins A, B-6, B-12, and E; folic acid, lysine, calcium phosphate, magnesium oxide, sulfate, and copper sulfate.

NIACIN, VITAMIN B-3

Abram Hoffer, MD, PhD, the father of Orthomolecular Psychiatry, noted that, if all the vitamin B-3 were removed from our food, everyone would become psychotic. The pandemic psychosis would resemble both pellagra and schizophrenia. Pellagra is a dietary deficiency disease caused by a lack of niacin, vitamin B-3, as discovered in 1937. Early in the last century about 10% of the patients in some insane asylums were suffering from this disease. Once a small amount of niacin was required to be added to wheat flour and other cereals used to make bread, pellagra became a rare disease in this country.

Dr Hoffer believes that, if a larger amount of this vitamin were added to flour, perhaps one gram per pound, the incidence of the more prevalent mental disease, schizophrenia, would drop significantly. About 1% of Americans are schizophrenic and 4 or 5% may be affected with less serious schizophrenic spectrum diseases. Most schizophrenics are released into the general population on medication. Some who have gone off their medication have committed serious crimes. Adding a little more niacin to our bread might make a big dent in a $50 billion per year problem!

One major reason we are not getting the benefits of scientific advances in nutrition is that few physicians have the requisite knowledge, and many have no interest in the subject. Dr. Williams, in his newsletter *Alternatives,* has noted that medical schools generally do not provide their students with an adequate education in nutrition. I recall an intern at Georgetown University Hospital telling me that taking supplemental vitamin C was permitting me to make expensive urine. After I informed him that most animals made lots of it internally, which humans are unable to do, and increased production when under stress, he said he would have to rethink his position.

In 1869, the <u>New York Medical Record</u> reported that the profession was inclined to discourage original thinking among its members. Also that originality of thought is discouraged in medical schools. In 2009, a retired physician told me that, when he was in medical school, he found that students who asked too many questions didn't graduate. Evidently, conforming to the ideas of respected authorities like the AMA and FDA is encouraged.

It is quite evident that a great many Americans are not in such good shape. The prevalence of overweight people and ubiquitous type II diabetes, which is even showing up in children, raises an important question: are changes in our food supply related to changes in our health?

IODINE

According to Dr. Bruce West's *Health Alert* of December 2005, Iodine used to be added to bread 20 years ago because it was considered to be deficient in people's diets. Iodine is present in every organ and tissue of the body and it is especially important in the thyroid gland. Dr. West claims that from 1900 to 1960 most physicians in the United States used iodine in the form of Lugol's solution for both hyper and hypo thyroidism, as well as many other diseases. Albert Szent Gyorgyi, MD, the discoverer of vitamin C, also noted that, when he was in medical school, physicians commonly prescribed potassium iodide when they didn't know what else to do. Presently bromine is added to bread instead of iodine. Bromine displaces iodine and has toxic effects on the thyroid gland which controls metabolism and hence might well be responsible for some people gaining too much weight. Fluorine, added to many municipal water supplies, also displaces iodine.

Guy Abraham, MD, former professor of endocrinology and an expert on medical use of iodine, claims that unwarranted fear of iodine by the medical profession has wreaked havoc on both the practice of medicine and patients. He feels that a great deal of unnecessary misery and death has resulted from this fear.

According to Dr. Bruce West, orthoiodo-supplementation, the provision or optimal amounts of iodine, is a panacea for a considerable number of disease conditions such as: fibrocystic breast disease, polycystic ovary syndrome, brain fog, obesity, diabetes, hypertension, and atria fibrillation. Is it possible that insufficient dietary iodine has contributed to the increasing prevalence of breast cancer, diabetes, high blood pressure, obesity, and thyroid cancer during the last 20 years?

FOOD AND SEXUAL CHARACTERISTICS

The recently published Textbook of Bio-Identical Hormones, by Edward M. Lichten, MD, contains some shocking news. American men have significantly deteriorated over the last half century. Blood testosterone level is an important indicator of male qualities like strength and aggressiveness. In the 1950's blood testosterone ranged between 400 and 1,200 nanograms per deciliter (ng/dl). Since then, average levels have been declining. In 2007, in the *Journal of Clinical Endocrinology and Metabolism*, Travison reported that the rate of decline has been about 1% per year for the last 20 years. Sperm counts have also dropped. Dr. Lichten notes that what he calls 'men-pause' is happening earlier and is accompanied by killing diseases. The incidence of diabetes was 1 in 150 in 1950; it is 1 in 30 now.

Intellectual capabilities of boys and young men have also decreased. Boyd Haley, PhD, head of the Chemistry Department of the University of Kentucky reported at a meeting of Doctors for Disaster Preparedness that boys have lost ground in math and science, and points have to be added to their test scores to get enough of them into law and medical schools.

In a report commissioned by the CHEM Trust, British biology Professor Richard Sharpe writes that rates of testicular cancer in young men are increasing. Furthermore, 7% of British boys are born with partly descended testes and about 7 in 1,000 have malformed genitals. He links the feminization of British boys and increased incidence of testicular cancer to chemicals found in food, cosmetics, and cleaning products. Numerous animal studies have shown that such substances are capable of modifying testosterone and producing testicular pathogenesis syndrome (TDS [26]) symptoms. This condition, which encompasses a number of male reproductive system abnormalities, has become a notable problem in that country. W. C. Douglas, MD, editor of the *Douglas Report*, says that it is also a problem in America. Reproductive anomalies are not confined to America and Great Britain. Twice as many girls as boys are born in heavily polluted areas of Canada, Italy, and Russia.

Along with the deterioration of men has come a substantial change in women. They are getting higher grades in mathematics and science than men and expanding their participation in the labor force. Some are presidents of Ivy League schools. They are maturing earlier, some experiencing menarche at age five, and they are becoming much more aggressive. Recently, a group of school girls bullied a schoolmate so much that she committed suicide.

---

[26] Also called testicular dysgenesis syndrome.

It is reasonable to believe that soy protein, 100 grams of which was determined to be the estrogenic equivalent of eleven birth control pills in a Swiss study, and baby bottles of soy milk, which have been estimated to contain the estrogenic equivalent of five birth control pills, might have something to do with the rise of women and the decline of men. Additionally, phthalates, which are found in many Plastics, and bis phenol A are said to influence sexual development of children. A recent study indicated that bis phenol A, in cash register and credit card receipts, when handled by pregnant women, can result in male children who are less aggressive than normal and female children who are more aggressive.

Lichten suggests that our food supply has significantly diminished nutritional value as well, and that it is necessary to supplement it with vitamins and minerals. Minerals and vitamins are needed for every chemical reaction in the body. He suggests about 5 to 10 times as much as the RDAs specify. Those with genetic defects require even more. In this connection readers should note that the international effort, via <u>Codex Alimentarious</u>, to limit the number and amounts of supplements procurable without a prescription, would make following Licten's recommendations difficult. Under <u>Codex</u> these vitamins and minerals would have to be prescription items likely to be very expensive.

A STEP ON THE ROAD TO FDA CONTROL OF DIETARY SUPPLEMENTS

Attempts to make the <u>Codex</u>, supported by FDA policies, a part of our legal system have been unsuccessful so far, even though required by our membership in the World Trade Organization and other international organizations.

A bill passed by Congress and signed into law by President Bush on 25 December, 2006, requires manufacturers of supplements to report adverse reactions to their products to the FDA. This expansion of power may be the first step on the road to the imposition of the <u>Codex Alimentarious</u> on Americans.

Passage of the bill may have been facilitated by statements such as that made recently by Dr. Alexander M. Walker, chairman of the Epidemiology Department of the Harvard School of Public Health. He estimates that less than 1% of serious adverse reactions are reported to the FDA and that the true proportions might be an order of magnitude less, i.e., 0.1%.

Since 1983, the Poison Control Center has collected statistics on adverse reactions ascribed to dietary supplements. In 23 years, they have caused about 1.6 million reactions, 251,799 hospitalizations and 230 deaths. In 1983, 14,006 adverse reactions were reported, and in 2005 there were 125,595. Reactions to vitamins, minerals, essential oils, herbs, and other materials were included in these totals. In 2005, ordinary vitamins were responsible for 64,446 reports (48,604 involving children less than six years old) and one death, minerals for 32,098 reports and 13 deaths, herbs for 23,769 and 13 deaths, and essential oils for 7,282 reports and no deaths. People have also died because they drank too much water!

Ten deaths per year from supplements in 23 years compares favorably with the record for drugs. During the last 30 years, the yearly death toll from drugs properly prescribed and taken has averaged about 100,000: another 80,000 from drugs improperly prescribed and taken, according to the *New England Journal of Medicine*. FDA's concern about the safety of supplements would seem to be unwarranted.

Accompanying this barrage of statistics, the National Center for Complementary and Alternative Medicine reports spending millions of dollars finding that six of the leading supplements provide no benefits to users. Possibly, this is a tribute to the well-established ability of the medical profession to design experiments to fail. Numerous other tests of these same supplements reached the opposite conclusion.

Presently, the FDA is very much concerned with tart cherries. They have warned cherry growers not to tell their customers about the promising results of scientific research which indicates that these cherries can provide many health benefits. They threaten to classify these cherries as drugs requiring multi-million dollar tests to prove that they are safe and effective. Do they fear that cherries might reduce profits of drug companies, to the point where they could no longer provide the FDA with $300 to 400 million a year to pay their bills?

Evidently, Congress is assisting the already wealthy pharmaceutical industry to limit competition from supplements. In 2010, Senators were still trying to hobble the food supplements industry. If the <u>Codex Alimentarious</u> becomes law, Americans will become sicker, and the pharmaceutical industry richer. Just limiting the availability of vitamin C and D-3 to RDA amounts will have this effect.

CHAPTER 10 - FREEDOM OF CHOICE IN MEDICAL CARE

Freedom of choice in medical care was taken for granted in the early days of our republic. However, Dr. Benjamin Rush, a prominent Philadelphia physician and signer of the Declaration of Independence, foresaw a need for its continuance. In 1787, he proposed that it be ensconced in our Constitution as recorded in the following statement:

> *"The Constitution of this Republic should make special provision for medical freedom. To restrict the art of healing to one class will constitute the Bastille of medical science. All such laws are un-American and despotic... Unless we put medical freedom into the Constitution; the time will come when medicine will organize into an undercover dictatorship and force people, who wish doctors and treatments of their own choice, to submit to only what the dictating outfit offers."*

What he foresaw has come to pass. We have a 100-year-old undercover dictatorship which forces people to take what the dictating outfit offers. The dictatorship has driven the costs of medical care to levels that threaten to bankrupt not only individuals, but businesses, states, and the Federal government. It discourages competition, and suppresses advances in medical science that promise to increase efficiency and reduce costs.

Jonathon Wright, in his September 2005 medical letter also agreed that, "despite the Constitution, we do not have freedom of choice in healthcare." He noted that a significant proportion of the half million annual American cancer deaths could be avoided if advances in technology such as the Rife Ray Machine and Dr. Stanislaw Burzinski's Antineoplastons were widely available. In 2010, we still do not have freedom of choice in medical care. If anything we have less than we had five years ago because insurance company clerks and computer programs have increasing influence over the practice of medicine.

Too many Americans die every year because of iatrogenic diseases and medical errors. Reports indicate that properly prescribed medications are killing 100,000 of us yearly. This is about the same rate as we lost soldiers during World War II. It was also reported in the *New England Journal of Medicine* that an additional 80,000 die from the effect of medications improperly prescribed and/or taken. Furthermore, another 100,000 yearly deaths are caused by drug resistant microorganisms. These facts indicate that we have a disaster on our hands. It is exacerbated by the 700,000 bankruptcies a year resulting from medical expenses.

Medical costs are adversely affecting businesses, and their ability to provide jobs. Some people have to choose between buying food and buying prescribed medications. Additionally, Medicare and Medicaid programs have big problems which can only become worse as the Baby Boomers retire during the next 20 years. Medical care is reported to have deteriorated to third world levels in some areas of the country.

In the past, a number of advancements in medical science have occurred which promised to benefit patients at reduced cost. Invariably, their developers have been given a hard time. Some of them were forced to leave the country. The biggest impediment to the introduction of advancements in medical science has been the medical-industrial establishment, which is, in effect, a monopoly and has long been standing in the way of freedom of choice.

The key to reductions in costs and improvements in quality of medical care lies in use of the many advancements in medical science which the monopoly has suppressed during the last 100 years. From a scientific point of view, recovering many of these technologies should not be difficult. However, potential political and legal roadblocks promise to make such recovery almost impossible in my lifetime.

The fact that a bill called the "Access to Medical Treatment Act" [27] has been introduced in Congress

---

27 See Appendix 4.

every year since 1996, without ever coming to a vote, provides a clear picture of the intent of Congress to maintain the monopoly it put in place at the beginning of the last century. Powerful interests which supply large sums of money for re-election campaigns are opposed to change. There is little chance that politicians, whose primary focus is on re-election, will act against the interests of their benefactors. A new approach is needed.

The fact that the *Fitzgerald Report* [28], commissioned in 1953, by Senator Tobey, then Chairman of the Interstate Commerce Commission, still lies buried in the <u>Congressional Record</u> confirms the unwillingness of Congress to investigate medical monopoly transgressions. Senator Bricker, who succeeded Tobey on the latter's death in 1953, refused to investigate the flagrant violations of law, and suppressions of advances in medical science which Fitzgerald uncovered. Benedict F. Fitzgerald, who made the investigation on which the report was based, was told to forget it and he would be taken care of. When he persisted in getting it into the <u>Congressional Record</u>, his job at the Justice Department disappeared.

What Dr. Rush did not foresee in 1787 was the abuse of political power by the undercover dictatorship which permits inoculation of children with dangerous materials against the wishes of their parents, and the

---

[28] See Appendix 2.

hooking of schizophrenic and bipolar patients on neuroleptic drugs, when the historical record shows that they are curable. It may also be responsible for the deterioration in reproductive capabilities of American men over the last 50 years, and the increase in degenerative diseases. Freedom of choice in medical care will terminate abuse of power by the undercover dictatorship.

Constitutional protection of the natural right to freedom of choice in medical care, which Dr. Benjamin Rush recommended in 1787, is needed even more in 2011, when international efforts to limit access to food supplements required to make up deficiencies in our food are increasing.

With this in mind the **FREEDOM OF CHOICE IN HEALTH CARE FOUNDATION** was formed in March 2010 to focus attention on the availability and need for higher quality and lower cost medical services. We invite all Americans to join with us in an effort to enact a Dr. Benjamin Rush Amendment [29] to the Bill of Rights of every state constitution and the Constitution for the United States in order to provide freedom of choice in medical care for ourselves and our Posterity. Since history shows that we cannot depend on

---

[29] Go to www.rush2013.com for information on The Dr. Benjamin Rush Amendment Project.

Congress to act on this issue, let us look to the individual States to act on our behalf.

SAMPLE Drafts of Proposed Amendments:

Federal Bill of Rights:
"The People of the United States of America and anyone lawfully residing or sojourning therein shall have freedom of choice and practice of any health or medical care modality as they deem in their own personal best interest and judgment."

State Bill of Rights:
"The People and any lawful inhabitant, resident, or sojourner of the state of (Your state) shall have freedom of choice and practice of any health or medical care modality as they deem in their own personal best interest and judgment."

APPENDIX 1. - The Hippocratic Oath

(Original Version)

I SWEAR by Apollo the physician, AEsculapius, and Health, and All-heal, and all the gods and goddesses, that, according to my ability and judgment, I will keep this Oath and this stipulation.

TO RECHON him who taught me this Art equally dear to me as my parents, to share my substance with him, and relieve his necessities if required; to look up his offspring in the same footing as my own brothers, and to teach them this art, if they shall wish to learn it, without fee or stipulation; and that by precept, lecture, and every other mode of instruction, I will impart a knowledge of the Art to my own sons, and those of my teachers, and to disciples bound by a stipulation and oath according the law of medicine, but to none others.

I WILL FOLLOW that system of regimen which, according to my ability and judgment, I consider for the benefit of my patients, and abstain from whatever is deleterious and mischievous. I will give no deadly medicine to any one if asked, nor suggest any such counsel; and in like manner I will not give a woman a pessary to produce abortion.

WITH PURITY AND WITH HOLINESS I will pass my life and practice my Art. I will not cut persons laboring under the stone, but will leave this to be done by men who are practitioners of this work. Into whatever houses I enter, I will go into them for the benefit of the sick, and will abstain from every voluntary act of mischief and corruption; and, further from the seduction of females or males, of freemen and slaves.

WHATEVER, IN CONNECTION with my professional practice or not, in connection with it, I see or hear, in the life of men, which ought not to be spoken of abroad, I will not divulge, as reckoning that all such should be kept secret.

WHILE I CONTINUE to keep this Oath unviolated, may it be granted to me to enjoy life and the practice of the art, respected by all men, in all times! But should I trespass and violate this Oath, may the reverse be my lot!

The Hippocratic Oath
(Modern Version)

I SWEAR in the presence of the Almighty and before my family, my teachers and my peers that according to my ability and judgment I will keep this Oath and Stipulation.

TO RECKON all who have taught me this art equally dear to me as my parents and in the same spirit and dedication to impart a knowledge of the art of medicine to others. I will continue with diligence to keep abreast of advances in medicine. I will treat without exception all who seek my ministrations, so long as the treatment of others is not compromised thereby, and I will seek the counsel of particularly skilled physicians where indicated for the benefit of my patient.

I WILL FOLLOW that method of treatment which according to my ability and judgment, I consider for the benefit of my patient and abstain from whatever is harmful or mischievous. I will neither prescribe nor administer a lethal dose of medicine to any patient even if asked nor counsel any such thing nor perform the utmost respect for every human life from fertilization to natural death and reject abortion that deliberately takes a unique human life.

WITH PURITY, HOLINESS AND BENEFICENCE I will pass my life and practice my art. Except for the prudent correction of an imminent danger, I will neither treat any patient nor carry out any research on any human being without the valid informed consent of the subject or the appropriate legal protector thereof, understanding that research must have as its purpose the furtherance of the health of that individual. Into whatever patient setting I enter, I will go for the benefit of the sick and will abstain from every voluntary act of mischief or corruption and further from the seduction of any patient.

WHATEVER IN CONNECTION with my professional practice or not in connection with it I may see or hear in the lives of my patients which ought not be spoken abroad, I will not divulge, reckoning that all such should be kept secret.

WHILE I CONTINUE to keep this Oath unviolated may it be granted to me to enjoy life and the practice of the art and science of medicine with the blessing of the Almighty and respected by my peers and society, but should I trespass and violate this Oath, may the reverse by my lot.

APPENDIX 2. - 1953 FITZGERALD REPORT

1953 FITZGERALD REPORT - SUPPRESSED CANCER TREATMENTS,

FROM THE CONGRESSIONAL RECORD

Introduction and comments on the Fitzgerald Report are taken from an article provided by Chris Gupta: www.newmediaexplorer.org/chris

Article Date: April 04, 2007

Introduction to the Report:
"In the 1950's, Congressman Charles Tobey enlisted Benedict Fitzgerald, an investigator for the Interstate Commerce Commission, to investigate allegations of conspiracy* and monopolistic practices on the part of orthodox medicine. This came about as the result of the son of Senator Tobey who developed cancer and was given less than two years to live by orthodox medicine. However, Tobey Jr., discovered options in the alternative field, received alternative treatment and fully recovered from his cancerous condition! That is when he learned of alleged conspiratorial practices on the part of orthodox medicine. He passed the word to his father, Senator Charles Tobey, who initiated an investigation. The final report clearly indicated there

was indeed a conspiracy to monopolize the medical and drug industry and to eliminate alternative options.

The "Fitzgerald Report" was submitted into the Congressional Record Appendix, August 3, 1953.

> *We are conditioned to think that conspiracies are only conjectures and the domain of the lunatic fringe - when a conspiracy is nothing but another name for <u>cartels</u> , monopolies, cabals, combines etc. This is simply another bait and switch tactic to confuse us from seeing the truth. [QUOTE: Chris Gupta]

> "One issue modern, orthodox medicine still fails to accept or take seriously, is "cause" and "maintenance." That is to deal not just with surgery of sick tissue; but to deal with the cause of the problem, to try to prevent it in the first place; and, further, to try to prevent it from recurring!" [30]

Instead of acting on the report to resolve the serious shortcomings found in mainstream medicine *The Fitzgerald Report* was suppressed for 53 years. "Suggest

---

[30] Extracted from: <u>Royal R. Rife</u>, by Gerald F. Foye, <u>ISBN 0-9659613-3-8</u>

you read the report below, then try to obtain a copy through regular channels."

"My investigation to date should convince this committee that a conspiracy does exist to stop the free flow and use of drugs in interstate commerce which allegedly has solid therapeutic value. Public and private funds have been thrown around like confetti at a country fair to close up and destroy clinics, hospitals, and scientific research laboratories which do not conform to the viewpoint of medical associations."

Benedict F. Fitzgerald, Jr., Special Counsel, US Senate Committee on Interstate and Foreign Commerce, 1953 [1]

1. Hon. William Langer, Congressional Record, August 3, 1953, p. A 5352.

Thanks to the tireless work of <u>Dr. Stan Monteith</u> who unearthed this seminal work. See his <u>January 2007 newsletter</u> for most enlightening comments.

Here, yet again, is another manifestation of power and privilege of a few at the expense of the many! This, at worst, is an apt description of democracy - while at best - it is mob rule where the many smother the few. Like the <u>sickness industry billed as health care</u> , democracy is billed as a utopian system. A system, which is supposed to defend our freedoms when itself it is anything but free. And has often been classic stepping stone to fascism.

I should hasten to add, that the following comments

are in no way to belittle the work of many thousands of hard working doctors and associated medical care professionals, who in the main, like the public, are themselves manipulated to conform to our current medical system. Those brave, courageous, and heroic souls who do try to improve matters and/or buck the system are swiftly dealt with as per the said report. There clearly are those who have different agendas as so aptly outlined in Dr. Stan Monteith's newsletter above.

This report is a hard hitting and deserved condemnation of the medical system with names, organizations and all, that has not changed to this day but has only become worse hence, this disclosure is even more credible today then it was in its own day - Reading it will drive home the reality of the situation we face. The transcript below is embellished with appropriate links. It will remove any doubts as to the dismal lack of safety and efficacy of mainstream cancer treatments to this day. Treatments themselves that are known to be <u>carcinogenic.</u> The most dangerous aspect about this, particularly to the unsuspecting, is the delay time, that can range from a few months to over 20 years, for cancer to manifest from the exposure to such primitive and mindless treatments. Furthermore, it is abundantly clear, as shown in the <u>vaccine shenanigans</u> , that there is in fact no intention to cure disease when common sense measures such as prevention, cause, whether <u>nutritional</u> and/or <u>environmental</u> are intentionally ignored.

(signed) Chris Gupta

Note:

Due to the importance of this find I have created and uploaded an excellent 35 minute computer generated audio of the report and the original photo copy of the report. They can be found here: http://www.newmediaexplorer.org/chris/index.htm.

Unfortunately, many transcript indices are not available at this time. Hopefully these can be found at a later date. However, many of the treatments discussed in this report can be found in the excellent book: Politics in Healing: The Suppression & Manipulation of American Medicine. CG

The Fitzgerald Report -1953

A Report by Special Counsel for a United States Senate Investigating Committee ... Making a Fact Finding Study of a Conspiracy against the Health of the American people.

THE UNDERSIGNED, as Special Counsel to the Senate Interstate and Foreign Commerce Committee, was directed to supervise a study of the following:

1. All those individuals, organizations, foundations, hospitals and clinics, throughout the United States, which have an effect upon interstate commerce and which have been conducting researches, investigations, experiments and demonstrations relating to the cause, prevention, and methods of

diagnosis and treatment of the disease cancer, to determine the interstate ramifications of their operations, their financial structures, including their fund-raising methods, and the amounts expended for clinical research as distinguished from administrative expenditures, and to ascertain the extent of the therapeutic value claimed by each in the use of its particular therapy.

2. The facts involving the discovery of, the imports from a foreign country of, the researches upon, and the interstate experiments, demonstrations, and use of the various drugs, preparations, and remedies for the treatment of the disease cancer, such drugs to include the so-called wonder drug Krebiozen, Glyoxylide, Mucorhicin and others.

3. The facts involving the interstate conspiracy, if any, engaged in by any individuals, organizations, corporations, associations, and combines of any kind whatsoever, to hinder, suppress, or restrict the free flow or transmission of Krebiozen, Glyoxylide, and Mucorhicin, and other drugs, preparations and remedies, and information, researches, investigations, experiments and demonstrations relating to the cause, prevention and methods of diagnosis and treatment of the disease cancer.

4. The facts involving the operations of voluntary cooperative prepaid medical plans and the organizations sponsoring said plans which are engaged in interstate commerce and which include in their programs medical treatment for the disease cancer, to determine the extent of their interstate

insurance operations, the identity of their originators and sponsors, and the resistance, if any, that each insurer has experienced from any individuals, organizations, corporations, associations, or combines, in their attempts to offer protection to those who are afflicted with the disease cancer.

5. The facts involving the inequality of opportunity, if any, that exists with regard to race, creed or color, in connection with the admission of students, researchers, and patients to institutions throughout the United States engaged in cancer therapy

<u>Activity Report</u>

Pursuant to the above, the undersigned commenced a collection and study of material covering the operations of foundations, hospitals, clinics, and government sponsored organizations specializing in cancer problems, including the following:

American Cancer Society
American Medical Association
Anne Fuller Fund, New Haven, Connecticut
Babe Ruth Foundation
Black, Stevenson Cancer Foundation, Hattiesburg, Mississippi
Bondy Fund, New York
Jonathan Bowman Fund, Madison, Wisconsin
Crocker Cancer Research Fund, New York
Damon Runyon Cancer Fund
Phillip L. Drosnes and the Drosnes-Lazenbey Clinic, Pittsburgh, Pa.
Dr. F. M. Eugene, Blass Clinic, Long Valley, New Jersey.

Government Organizations:

The Department of Health, Education and Welfare
a. Food and Drug Administration
b. Federal Trade Commission
Dr. Gregory Clinic, Pasadena, California
Hoxsey Cancer Clinic, 4507 Gaston Avenue, Dallas, Texas
C. P. Huntington Fund, New York
International Cancer Research Foundation, Philadelphia, Pa.
John Hopkins Hospital, Baltimore, Md.
Dr. Waldo Jones, Myrtle Beach, South Carolina
Dr. William F. Koch and Rev. Sam Swain Clinic, also known
as the Christian Medical Research League, Detroit, Michigan
and Brazil, South America
Lakeland Foundation, Chicago, Illinois
Lincoln Foundation , Medford, Mass.
Memorial Hospital, New York
Dr. K. F. Murphy and Dr. Charles Lyman Lofler Clinic, 25 E.
Washington Street, Chicago, Illinois
New York Skin and Cancer Hospital, New York
Radium Institute of New York
Henry Rutherford Fund, New York
Charles F. Spang Foundation, Pittsburgh, Pa.
University of Chicago, Chicago, Illinois
University of Illinois, Champaign, Illinois

Thereafter, the undersigned travelled to Illinois to
investigate the so-called Krebiozen controversy, and
on July 2, 1953, wrote a report on his findings which is
attached hereto and marked "Exhibit A." Included in
this report was the evaluation:

"The controversy is involved and requires further
research and development. There is reason to believe
that the AMA has been hasty, capricious, arbitrary,

247

and outright dishonest, and of course if the doctrine of 'respondeat superior' is to be observed, the alleged machinations of Dr. J. J. Moore (for the past ten years the treasurer of the AMA) could involve the AMA and others in an interstate conspiracy of alarming proportions. "

"The principal witnesses who tell of Dr. Moore's rascality are Alberto Barreira, Argentine cabinet member, and his secretary, Anna D. Schmidt."

Thereafter, the undersigned visited other areas, interrogating medical men, and on July 14, 1953, wrote a further report. Included in this was the evaluation:

"Being vitally interested and having tried to listen and observe closely, it is my profound conviction that this substance Krebiozen is one of the most promising materials yet isolated for the management of cancer. It is biologically active. I have gone over the records of 530 cases, most of them conducted at a distance from Chicago, by unbiased cancer experts and clinics. In reaching my conclusions I have of course discounted my own lay observations and relied mostly on the opinions of qualified cancer research workers and ordinary experienced physicians.

"I have concluded that in the value of present cancer research, this substance and the theory behind it deserves the most full and complete and scientific study. Its value in the management of the cancer patient has been demonstrated in a sufficient number and percentage of cases to demand further work.

"Behind and over all this is the weirdest conglomeration of corrupt motives, intrigue, selfishness, jealousy, obstruction and conspiracy that I have ever seen."

"Dr. Andrew C. Ivy , who has been conducting research upon this drug, is absolutely honest intellectually, scientifically, and in every other way. Moreover, he appears to be one of the most competent and unbiased cancer experts that I have ever come in contact with, having served on the board of the American Cancer Society and the American Medical Association and in that capacity having been called upon to evaluate various types of cancer therapy. Dr. George G. Stoddard, President of the University of Illinois, in assisting in the cessation of Dr. Ivy's research on cancer at the University of Illinois, and in recommending the abolishment of the latter's post as Vice President of that institution, has in my opinion shown attributes of intolerance for scientific research in general."

It is a matter of common knowledge that the entire subject matter is highly controversial and thus further and additional research and development would entail more time. A controversy among renowned Surgeons, Pathologists, Cancerologists and Radiologists should not deter or silence this Committee from carrying out the mandate contemplated and expressly directed by the late Chairman of your Committee, Senator Charles W. Tobey, by virtue of the resolution passed by the Senate.

Now, passing on to another institution, I have very

carefully studied the court records of three cases tried in the Federal and State Courts of Dallas, TX. A running fight has been going on between officials, especially Dr. Morris Fishbein of the American Medical Association through the Journal of that organization, and the Hoxsey Cancer Clinic. Dr. Fishbein contended that the medicines employed by the Hoxsey Cancer Clinic had no therapeutic value; that it was run by a quack and a charlatan. (This clinic is manned by a staff of over 30 employees, including nurses and physicians). Reprints and circulation of several million copies of articles so prepared resulted in litigation. The Government thereafter intervened and sought an injunction to prevent the transmission in interstate commerce of certain medicines. It is interesting to note that in the Trial Court, before Judge Atwell, who had an opportunity to hear the witnesses in two different trials, it was held that the so-called Hoxsey method of treating cancer was in some respects superior to that of x-ray, radium and surgery and did have therapeutic value. The Circuit Court of Appeals of the 5th Circuit decided otherwise. This decision was handed down during the trial of a libel suit in the District Court of Dallas, TX, by Hoxsey against Morris Fishbein, who admitted that he had never practiced medicine one day in his life and had never had a private patient, which resulted in a verdict for Hoxsey and against Morris Fishbein. The defense admitted that Hoxsey could cure external cancer but contended that his medicines for internal cancer had no therapeutic value. The jury, after listening to leading Pathologists, Radiologists, Physicians, Surgeons and scores of witnesses, a great number of whom had never been treated by any Physician or

250

Surgeon except the treatment received at the Hoxsey Cancer Clinic, concluded that Dr. Fishbein was wrong; that his published statements were false, and that the Hoxsey method of treating cancer did have therapeutic value.

In this litigation the Government of the United States, as well as Dr. Fishbein, brought to the Court the leading medical scientists, including Pathologists and others skilled in the treatment of cancer. They came from all parts of the country. It is significant to note that a great number of these doctors admitted that x-ray therapy could cause cancer . This view is supported by medical publications, including the magazine entitled *CANCER* published by the American Cancer Society, May issue of 1948.

I am herewith including the names and addresses of some of the witnesses who testified in the State and Federal Court. It has been determined by pathology, in a great many instances by laboratories wholly disconnected from the Hoxsey Cancer Clinic, that they were suffering from different types of cancer, both internal and external, and following treatment they testified they were cured.

Name – Address - Type

J. A. Johnson Ranger, TX. Squamous Cell No. 2

Mrs. R. J. Hickman, 1225 E. Allen St. Ft. Worth, Tex
Melanocarcinoma

Robt. Thane Avoca,, TX. Myxoliposarcoma

Mrs. H. H. Johnson, Denton, TX. Adenocarcinoma

Mrs. Elmer Smith, Wellington, TX. Malignant Melanoma

Mildred Rager, 2101 Stovall St., Dallas TX. Melanoma

A. G. Burgess, 2416 Wyman St., Dallas TX. Basal Cell Carcinoma

Ira Poston, 5322 Victor St., Dallas TX. Basal Cell Carcinoma

W. E. Harmon, Grapevine, TX. Prickle Cell Carcinoma

Mrs. J. A. Robb, Weatherford, TX. Basal Cell Carcinoma

Mrs. Lessie Hester, Lubbock, TX. Adenocarcinoma of Uterus

Mrs. Lora Barnett, Peniel, TX. Adenocarcinoma of Uterus

Mrs. E. E. Hockett, Farmersville, TX. RFD Prickle Cell Carcinoma

T. E. Truman, Waco, TX. Epidermoid Carcinoma

Fritz Trojan, Waco, TX. Squamous Cell type

Mr. C. W. Malone, Brownwood, TX. Basal Cell type

Val Seurer, Hinton, Okla. Malignant Carcinoma

Jo Parelll Sportotorium, Dallas, TX. Malignant Carcinoma

Mrs. R. M. Hoffman, c-o J. B. Baird Co. Shreveport, La. Spindle Cell
Carcinoma

Tom Coates Merkel, TX. Basal Cell Carcinoma

J. L. Renfro, Merkel, TX. Malignant Carcinoma

Mrs. J. D. Douglas, Ft. Worth. TX. Duct-cell Carcinoma

Mrs. R. S. Turner, Carcinoma Grade 3 Squamous Cell

Mrs. C. E. Mallory, Squamous Cell Carcinoma

Mrs. Herman Thomas, 5222 Merrimac St., Dallas, TX.
Melanocarcinoma

Clifton H. Smith 5637 Hiram St., Ft. Worth, TX Malignant
Carcinoma

Rev. Horace W. Irwin, West Warwick, Rhode Island Malignant
Carcinoma

I have had access to literature by leading scientists
in the field of medicine. The attention of the
Committee is invited to the hearings held during
the 79th Congress, in July 1946; Senate Bill 1875

being under consideration, wherewith it appears, as follows:

"Dr. George Miley was born in Chicago, 1907, graduated from Chicago Latin School, 1923, graduated with B.A. from Yale University in 1927, from Northwestern Medical School, 1932, interned at Chicago Memorial Hospital in 1932 and 1933, University of Vienna Postgraduate Medical School, 1933, 1934, following which he visited the hospitals in India, China and Japan. He is a fellow of the American Association for the Advancement of Science. He holds a national board certificate and since 1945 he has been medical director of the Gotham Hospital, New York.

"Report of Dr. Miley of a survey made by Dr. Stanley Reimann (in charge of Tumor Research and Pathology, Gotham Hospital) before Senator Pepper's Committee on Senate Bill 1875, a bill to authorize expenditure of one hundred million dollars in cancer research.

"Dr. Reimann's report on cancer cases in Pennsylvania over a long period of time showed that those who received no treatment lived a longer period than those that received surgery, radium or x-ray. The exceptions were those patients who had received electro-surgery. The survey also showed that following the use of radium and x-ray much more harm than good was done to the average cancer patient."

"Dr. William Seaman Bainbridge, AM, ScD, MD,

253

CM, F.I.C.S. (Hon.) was the recipient of six honorary degrees from various institutions, the most recent being the degree of Doctor Honoris Cause from the University of San Marcos, Peru. He has been surgeon at the New York Skin and Cancer Hospital, Surgical Director of New York City Children's Hospital and of Manhattan State Hospital, Ward's Island, and consulting surgeon and gynecologist to various hospitals in the New York metropolitan and suburban areas.

"While there are some who still believe in the efficacy of radiation as a cure, my skepticism with regard to its value is being increasingly substantiated. But even with the best technic of today, its curative effect in real cancer is questionable." In 1939 the great British physiologist, Sir Leonard Hill, wrote: 'Large doses (of gamma and hard x-ray) produced destruction of normal tissues such as marrow and lymphoid tissue, leukocytes and epithelial linings, and death ensues ... The nation would, I think, be little the worse off if all the radium in the country now buried for security from bombing in deep holes, remains therein.'

"<u>A neoplasm should never be incised for diagnostic purposes, for one cannot tell at what split moment the cancer cells may be disseminated and the patient doomed</u>. Aspirating the neoplasm to draw out the cells by suction: this, too, is a very questionable procedure, for what of the cancer cells that may be present below the puncture point and around the needle which have been set free? It must be realized that while cancer cannot be transplanted from man to man, it can be transplanted in the same host." *

(* Although now we know that can in fact be transplanted from man to man. CG
See "Brain tumor linked to liver transplant:"
http://www.newmediaexplorer.org/chris/2003/06/27
/brain_tumor_linked_to_liver_transplant.htm)

"There is a report from another source in which Doctor Feinblatt, for six years Pathologist of the Memorial Hospital, New York, reported that the Memorial Hospital had originally given x-ray and radium treatment before and after radical operations for breast malignancy. These patients did not long survive, so x-ray and radium were given after surgery only. These patients lived a brief time only and after omitting all radiation, patients lived the longest of all." (See index)

Doctors Warned To Be Wary In Use Of X-Rays In Disease Treatment, by Howard W. Blakeslee, Associated Press Science Editor.

"New York, July 6, 1948 X-rays and gamma rays can cause bone cancer is warning issued in 'Cancer,' a new medical journal started by the American Cancer Society. The bone cancer warning, covering more than twenty pages, is by Doctors William G Cahan. Helen Q. Woodward, Norman L. Higgin-botham. Fred W. Steward and Bradlev I. Coley, all of New York City.

"One of the most dangerous things about this kind of bone cancer, the report states, is the very long delay between the use of the rays and the appearance of the cancers. The delay time in the eleven cases ranged from six to twenty-two years."

"Doctor Herman Joseph Muller, Nobel Prize Winner, a world renowned scientist, has stated the Medical Profession is permanently damaging the American life stream through the unwise use of x-rays. There is no dosage of x-ray so low as to be without risk of producing harmful mutations."

The attention of the Committee is invited to the request made by Senator Elmer Thomas following an investigation made by the Senator of the Hoxsey Cancer Clinic under date of February 25th, 1947, and addressed to the Surgeon General, Public Health Department, Washington, D.C., wherein he sought to enlist the support of the Federal Government to make an investigation and report. No such investigation was made. In fact, every effort was made to avoid and evade the investigation by the Surgeon General's office. The record will reveal that this clinic did furnish 62 complete case histories, including pathology, names of hospitals, physicians, etc., in 1945. Again in June, 1950, 77 case histories, which included the names of the patients, pathological reports in many instances, and in the absence thereof, the names of the Pathologists, hospitals and physicians who had treated these patients before being treated at the Hoxsey Cancer Clinic. The Council of National Cancer Institute, without investigation, in October

1950, refused to order an investigation. The record in the Federal Court discloses that this agency of the Federal Government took sides and sought in every way to hinder, suppress and restrict this institution in their treatment of cancer. (See testimony Dr. Gilcin Meadors, Pages 1125-1139 Transcript of Records, Case No. 13645, U.S.C.A.)

Among the numerous foundations and clinics which profess to possess a remedy for the treatment of cancer is the Lincoln Foundation of Medford, Massachusetts, which has been the particular target of the AMA. I have not had an opportunity to sufficiently explore the particular type of therapy employed by this institution. However, I understand it involves a unique theory of inhalant therapy and the transmission of bacteria-phage. In passing it is important to note that this technique was the subject of particular interest to the late Chairman who was a trustee of the Lincoln Foundation following a successful treatment of his son Charles W. Tobey, Jr. This remedy has been tried by hundreds of patients and it is alleged that these treatments have been proven beneficial.

Another institution which claims to have made some progress in the treatment of cancer is the Drosnes-Lazenbey Cancer Clinic of Pittsburgh, Pa. The reports would indicate that this institution is likewise entitled to a hearing before this Committee. The heavy toll of life being taken by cancer requires a searching investigation. The methods employed, as I understand it, is a substance known as Mucorhicin, which is reported to be of therapeutic value.

Under the fourth assignment concerning voluntary cooperative prepaid medical plans and any resistance encountered from organizations, associations or combines, it is a matter of public record in the Federal and State Court that medical associations have put up a road block whenever or wherever this is attempted.

The Committee on Labor and Public Welfare, through its Sub-Committee on Health, submitted the results of a study of health insurance plans in the United States, in a report issued in May 1951, 82nd Congress. This was accomplished under the direction of Dr. Dean H. Clark, now the Director of the Massachusetts General Hospital. This appears to be the first objective and impartial study of the scope, benefits and effectiveness of voluntary health insurance plans. It shows that one-half of the population at that time had some form of protection against the cost of hospital care, but three million had what can be called comprehensive protection against the cost of hospital and medical care. Specifically with reference to cancer, it would appear that an opportunity would be afforded members of this sort of a health program to periodic checkups to determine whether they had cancer. This subject was discussed at length between Kenneth Meiklejohn, Staff Director of the Sub-Committee on Health, and Senator Tobey two years ago. Correspondence between the two is available. The reports, of course, are available to the members of this Committee.

From a strictly legal as well as ethical approach, if one individual has the right to select his own physician or hospital, why cannot 10,000 individuals and their families determine that they intend to invest directly, or indirectly, in the construction and maintenance of a hospital, employ a staff of competent physicians, surgeons, technicians, laboratory experts, nurses, interns, et cetera, to look after their health problems? This is not so-called socialized medicine. It is purely voluntary. Here, as elsewhere stated in this report, the jurisdiction of the Committee may be limited. It may properly belong to the States and their legislators and courts to determine this problem. However, the general welfare clause of the Constitution may be the answer. If the Committee should determine that it has jurisdiction, I am of the opinion that competent legal evidence can be presented which will aid and assist the Committee in its final judgment.

With reference to the fifth assignment, you are advised that time did not permit me to ascertain the number of students or the increase thereof in the various medical schools throughout the country. It has been suggested that a studied effort has been made by certain groups to <u>keep the number of students enrolling in medical schools at a low figure</u> . I do not assert this to be the fact and I doubt if the Committee would have jurisdiction to go into that question. This would properly belong to the States. If this is a fact, then the various State legislatures of the country should, of course, take necessary steps, consistent with the public welfare, to see that every opportunity is given to any boy or girl who possesses the necessary qualifications to be permitted to enter medical schools. If, on the other hand, this Committee believes that it has jurisdiction under the General Welfare Clause of the Constitution to go forward, then certainly it would be a proper and timely matter of inquiry. In any event, you do have jurisdiction and should complete the investigation in so far as cancer is concerned by those engaged in the research field.

A careful study of the subject matter embraced in the direction of the late Chairman will disclose the tremendous importance of the investigation undertaken and the consideration of the results by the members of this Committee.

We have long since passed the age of witch hunting. We are, notwithstanding, living in an era of hysteria. Investigation seems to be the order of the day. Crude thinking results in hysterical action. Perhaps the converse is true. The beginning of hysteria is the end of sound thinking. Proceeding, therefore, to the end result sought by all, we recognize the value of our goal in striving for a sound, vigorous and healthful Nation at minimum costs. Money, however, lavishly spent to stamp out a dreadful scourge is sound public economy.

I have approached this problem with an open mind. Recognizing the importance of men skilled in the science of medicine, who are best informed, if not qualified, on the question of cancer, its causes and treatment, I directed my attention to the propaganda by the American Medical Association and the American Cancer Society to the effect: namely, "that radium, x-ray therapy, and surgery are the only recognized treatments for cancer."

Is there any dispute among recognized medical scientists in America and elsewhere in the world on the use of radium and x-ray therapy in the treatment of cancer? The answer is definitely "Yes," there is a division of opinion on the use of radium and x-ray. Both agencies are destructive, not constructive. In the alleged destruction of the abnormal, outlaw or cancer cells both x-ray therapy and radium destroy normal tissue and normal cells. Recognized medical authorities in America and elsewhere state positively that x-ray therapy can cause cancer in and of itself. ("This is true for Chemotherapy as well..." CG)

Chemotherapy is incapable of extending in any appreciable way the lives of patients afflicted with the most common cancers-and even the palliative effect of these toxic drugs, which supposedly improve the quality of life, "rests on scientifically shaky ground." That was the conclusion of West German cancer biostatistician Ulrich Abel, PhD, in the most comprehensive study ever undertaken on cancer chemotherapy. In his 1990 book Dr. Abel wrote, "There is no evidence for the vast majority of cancers that treatment with these drugs exerts any positive influence on survival or quality of life in patients with advanced disease." The advanced cancers to which Dr. Abel is referring are those malignancies responsible for over 80% of the cancer deaths in the Western industrial countries. "Among others, they include nearly all malignant tumors of trachea, bronchus, lung, stomach, colon, rectum, esophagus, breast, bladder, pancreas, ovary, cervix and corpus uteri, head and neck, and liver. Tumors are called advanced if they are recurrent, disseminated, or not radically resectable."

Extracted from: Options by Richard Walters

The increased number of cancer patients in America of all ages and the apparent failure to presently cope with this dreaded disease indicates the necessity of a sustained effort of private and Federal agencies to continue research in the field of cancer; its causes and treatment.

<u>If radium, x-ray or surgery or either of them is the complete answer, then the greatest hoax of the age is being perpetrated upon the people by the continued appeal for funds for further research</u> . If neither x-ray, radium or- surgery is the complete answer to this dreaded disease, and I submit that it is not, then what is the plain duty of society? Should we stand still? Should we sit idly by and count the number of physicians, surgeons and cancerologists who are not only divided but who, because of fear or favor, are forced to line up with the so-called accepted view of the American Medical Association, or should this Committee make a full scale investigation of the organized

effort to hinder, suppress and restrict the free flow of drugs which allegedly have proven successful in cases where clinical records, case history, pathological reports and x-ray photographic proof, together with the alleged cured patients, are available.

Accordingly, we should determine whether existing agencies, both public and private, are engaged and have pursued a policy of harassment, ridicule, slander and libelous attacks on others sincerely engaged in stamping out this curse of mankind. Have medical associations, through their officers, agents, servants and employees engaged in this practice? My investigation to date should convince this Committee that a conspiracy does exist to stop the free flow and use of drugs in interstate commerce which allegedly has solid therapeutic value. Public and private funds have been thrown around like confetti at a country fair to close up and destroy clinics, hospitals and scientific research laboratories which do not conform to the viewpoint of medical associations.

How long will the American people take this? To illustrate the stranglehold of the American Medical Association on legislation which in turn affects every household in America, let us look at a small 25 cent tube of penicillin ointment. Is it dangerous to have around the house for a cut or small bruise on your body? Rat poison can be bought without a doctor's prescription. The sale of arsenic must have a doctor's prescription. The sale of arsenic and rat poisons is small but not penicillin. Accordingly we must have a doctor's prescription in America to buy a 25 cent tube of ointment. In Canada, however, the Medical Association has not yet discovered THE GREAT DANGER of a small tube of penicillin ointment and, accordingly the people are able to buy it without paying a doctor for a prescription. To say that it is dangerous is silly. To assert, rather, that it is but another manifestation of power and privilege of a few at the expense of the many would be more consistent with truth and wholly accurate.

What is the duty of this Committee and the members thereof? Your first duty, of course, is to do right. Properly considered, that is your only duty. In doing right, however, you owe a duty to the American people. In upholding the law and enacting legislation for the people of America, we look first to the instrument of our creation as a representative form of Government. Those powers not specifically conferred upon the Federal Government and denied to the States, are reserved either to the States or to the people. Thus the founding fathers very wisely created an area of freedom in which free men shall function. **It is in this area set aside by the fathers of our Republic that people have the right to own property, transact business, build up a system of free enterprise without hindrance, harassment or abuse of either the Government, State or Federal, or of other citizens, however powerful, so long as the people so engaged do not trespass upon the rights of others.** This is the basic concept of liberty functioning in America. It may be said to be a reservoir of freedom. In this area we have mingled our money and blood with the races of mankind. We have demonstrated our ability to live together peacefully and happily, although we represent most of the races, most of the colors and most of the creeds. This was an innovation and a new experiment to the peoples of the old world. Out of and from this area has sprung the noblest dreams and saintliest purposes of mankind, purposes so strong and vital that it has become the envy and admiration of a waiting world. People look longingly to the shores of America and desire to make this their asylum of escape and hope for the future. It is more than a dream. It is a reality. While we have not solved all the problems of mankind, we have at least provided a sanctuary and the instruments of government, if properly guarded against the abuse of selfish men and organizations who would bend it to suit their purposes, which could live for centuries to come. In this connection this Committee should investigate the advertising agency which controls all advertising in the Journal of the American Medical Association as well as the various State Journals. Why is the stamp of approval, by the so-called nutrition expert and their Council on Foods, placed on certain foodstuffs, denied to others, and others condemned, without a reasonable investigation? Is there any relationship between approval by these experts and the operation of the advertising agency in the offices of the American Medical Association?

May I, with propriety, call your attention to the tragedy which has invaded the United States Senate. Four great Americans, all of them, Senator McMahon, Senator Wherry, Senator Vandenberg and

Senator Bob Taft were all stricken down with this dreaded disease. We are under a compelling moral obligation to the memory of these great public servants and to the untold millions of cancer sufferers throughout the world to carry on this investigation. We cannot do otherwise.

Respectfully submitted,
Benedict F. Fitzgerald
Special Counsel

APPENDIX 3. - Renowned Psychiatrist L. R. Mosher Resigns

http://www.critpsynet.freeuk.com/Mosher.htm

RENOWNED PSYCHIATRIST LOREN R. MOSHER RESIGNS FROM THE AMERICAN PSYCHIATRIC ASSOCIATION IN DISGUST

This is a copy of a letter by Dr. Mosher resigning from the American Psychiatric Association. Note that Dr. Mosher was a pioneer in establishing programs of psychosocial community care in the field of psychiatry (e.g., Soteria House,); his many publications in that regard have been very influential (e.g.: Mosher, L., & Burti, L. (1989). "Community Mental Health: Principles and Practice." New York: Norton.)

Loren R. Mosher M D
2616 Angell Ave.
San Diego, CA 92122

December 4 1998

Rodrigo Munoz, MD, President
American Psychiatric Association
1400 94 Street N W
Washington, D.C. 20005

Dear Rod;

After nearly three decades as a member it is with a mixture of pleasure and disappointment that I submit this letter of resignation from the American Psychiatric Association. The major reason for this action is my belief that I am actually resigning from the American Psychopharmacological Association. Luckily, the organization's true identity requires no change in the acronym.

Unfortunately, APA reflects, and reinforces, in word and deed, our drug dependent society. Yet, it helps wage war on drugs. Dual Diagnosis clients are a major problem for the field but not because of the good drugs we prescribe. Bad ones are those that are obtained mostly without a prescription. A Marxist would observe that being a good capitalist organization, APA likes only those drugs from which it can derive a profit - directly or indirectly.

This is not a group for me. At this point in history, in my view, psychiatry has been almost completely bought out by the drug companies. The APA could not continue without the pharmaceutical company support of meetings, symposia, workshops, journal advertising, grand rounds luncheons, unrestricted educational grants, etc. etc. Psychiatrists have become the minions of drug company promotions. APA, of course, maintains that its independence and autonomy are not compromised in this enmeshed situation.

Anyone with the least bit of common sense attending the annual meeting would observe how the drug company exhibits and industry sponsored symposia draw crowds with their various enticements while the serious scientific sessions are barely attended. Psychiatric training reflects their influence as well; i.e., the most important part of a resident curriculum is the art and quasi-science of dealing drugs, i.e., prescription writing.

These psychopharmacological limitations on our abilities to be complete physicians also limit our intellectual horizons. No longer do we seek to understand whole persons in their social contexts, rather we are there to realign our patients' neurotransmitters. The problem is that it is very difficult to have a relationship with a neurotransmitter whatever its configuration.

So, our guild organization provides a rationale, by its neurobiological tunnel vision, for keeping our distance from the molecule conglomerates we have come to define as patients. We condone and promote the widespread overuse and misuse of toxic chemicals that we know have serious long term effects: tardive dyskinesia, tardive dementia, and serious withdrawal syndromes. So, do I want to be a drug company patsy who treats molecules with their formulary? No, thank you very much. It saddens me that after 35 years as a psychiatrist I look forward to being dissociated from such an organization. In no way does it represent my interests. It is not within my capacities to buy into the current biomedical-reductionistic model heralded by the psychiatric leadership as once again marrying us to somatic medicine. This is a matter of fashion, politics and, like the pharmaceutical house connection, money.

In addition, APA has entered into an unholy alliance with NAMI (I don't remember the members being asked if they supported such an organization) such that the two organizations have adopted similar public belief systems about the nature of madness. While professing itself the champion of their clients the APA is supporting non-clients, the parents, in their wishes to be in control, via legally enforced dependency, of their mad/bad offspring. NAMI, with tacit APA approval, has set out a pro-neuroleptic drug and easy commitment-institutionalization agenda that violates the civil rights of their offspring. For the most part we stand by and allow this fascistic agenda to move forward. Their psychiatric god, Dr. E. Fuller Torrey, is allowed to diagnose and recommend treatment to those in the NAMI organization with whom he disagrees. Clearly, a violation of medical ethics. Does APA protest? Of course not, because he is speaking what APA agrees with but can't explicitly espouse. He is allowed to be a foil; after all he is no longer a member of APA. (Slick work APA!)

The shortsightedness of this marriage of convenience between APA, NAMI and the drug companies (who gleefully support both groups because of their shared pro-drug stance) is an abomination. I want no part of a psychiatry of oppression and social control.

Biologically based brain diseases are convenient for families and practitioners alike. It is no fault insurance against personal responsibility. We are just helplessly caught up in a swirl of brain pathology for which no one, except DNA, is responsible. Now, to begin with, anything that has an anatomically defined specific brain pathology becomes the province of neurology (syphilis is an excellent example). So, to be consistent with this "brain disease" view all the major psychiatric disorders would become the territory of our neurologic colleagues. Without having surveyed them

I believe they would eschew responsibility for these problematic individuals. However, consistency would demand our giving over "biologic brain diseases" to them. The fact that there is no evidence confirming the brain disease attribution is, at this point, irrelevant. What we are dealing with here is fashion, politics and money. This level of intellectual/scientific dishonesty is just too egregious for me to continue to support by my membership.

I view with no surprise that psychiatric training is being systemically disavowed by American medical school graduates. This must give us cause for concern about the state of today's psychiatry. It must mean, at least in part, that they view psychiatry as being very limited and unchallenging. To me it seems clear that we are headed toward a situation in which, except for academics, most psychiatric practitioners will have no real relationships, so vital to the healing process, with the disturbed and disturbing persons they treat. Their sole role will be that of prescription writers, ciphers in the guise of being "helpers."

Finally, why must the APA pretend to know more than it does? DSM IV is the fabrication upon which psychiatry seeks acceptance by medicine in general. Insiders know it is more a political than scientific document. To its credit it says so, although its brief apologia is rarely noted. DSM IV has become a bible and a money making best seller - its major failings notwithstanding. It confines and defines practice, some take it seriously, others more realistically. It is the way to get paid. Diagnostic reliability is easy to attain for research projects. The issue is what do the categories tell us? Do they in fact accurately represent the person with a problem? They don't, and can't, because there are no external validating criteria for psychiatric diagnoses. There is neither a blood test nor specific anatomic lesions for any major psychiatric disorder. So, where are we? APA as an organization has implicitly (sometimes explicitly as well) bought into a theoretical hoax. Is psychiatry a hoax, as practiced today?

What do I recommend to the organization upon leaving after experiencing three decades of its history?

1. To begin with, let us be ourselves. Stop taking on unholy alliances without the members' permission.

2. Get real about science, politics and money. Label each for what it is - that is, be honest.

3. Get out of bed with NAMI and the drug companies. APA should align itself, if one believes its rhetoric, with the true consumer groups, i.e., the ex-patients, psychiatric survivors etc.

4. Talk to the membership; I can't be alone in my views.

We seem to have forgotten a basic principle: the need to be patient/client/consumer satisfaction oriented. I always remember Manfred Bleuler's wisdom: "Loren, you must never forget that you are your patient's employee." In the end they will determine whether or not psychiatry survives in the service marketplace.

Sincerely,
Loren R. Mosher M. D.

APPENDIX 4. - ACCESS TO MEDICAL TREATMENT ACT

H.R.746

Access to Medical Treatment Act

(Introduced in the House)

105th CONGRESS
1st Session
H. R. 746
To allow patients to receive any medical treatment they want under certain conditions, and for other purposes.

IN THE HOUSE OF REPRESENTATIVES
February 13, 1997

Mr. DEFAZIO (for himself, Mr. BARTON of TX, Mr. KILDEE, Mr. ABERCROMBIE, Mr. DELLUMS, Mr. SANDERS, Mr. EVANS, Mr. HINCHEY, Mr. PICKETT, Mr. HAYWORTH, Mr. STUMP, Ms. NORTON, Mr. ARCHER, Mr. OWENS, Mrs. CHENOWETH, Mr. CLEMENT, Mr. CONDIT, Mr. CAMPBELL, Mr. RAHALL, Mr. MCGOVERN, Mr. MCDERMOTT, Mr. ROHRABACHER, Mr. MORAN of Virginia, Mr. ANDREWS, Mr. FOGLIETTA, Mr. HEFLEY, Ms. WOOLSEY, Mr. COX of California, Mr. PALLONE, Ms. FURSE, Mr. ACKERMAN, Mr. DREIER, Mr. FALEOMAVAEGA, Ms. JACKSON-LEE of TX, Mr. GRAHAM, Mr. RUSH, Mr. TALENT, Mr. WYNN, Mr. FILNER, Mr. DEUTSCH, and Mr. BURTON of Indiana) introduced the following bill; which was referred to the

Committee on Commerce.

A BILL

To allow patients to receive any medical treatment they want under certain conditions, and for other purposes.

Be it enacted by the Senate and House of Representatives of the United States of America in Congress assembled:

SECTION 1. SHORT TITLE.

This Act may be cited as the `Access to Medical Treatment Act'.

SEC. 2. DEFINITIONS.

As used in this Act:

   (1) ADVERTISING CLAIMS- The term `advertising claims' means any representations made or suggested by statement, word, design, device, sound, or any combination thereof with respect to a medical treatment.

   (2) DANGER- The term `danger' means any negative reaction that--

      (A) causes serious harm;

      (B) occurred as a result of a method of medical treatment;

      (C) would not otherwise have occurred; and

      (D) is more serious than reactions experienced with routinely used medical treatments for the same medical condition or conditions.

   (3) DEVICE- The term `device' has the same meaning given such term in section 201(h) of the Federal Food, Drug, and Cosmetic Act (21 U.S.C. 321(h)).

   (4) DRUG- The term `drug' has the same meaning given such term in section 201(g)(1) of the Federal Food, Drug, and Cosmetic Act (21 U.S.C. 321(g)(1)).

   (5) FOOD- The term `food' —

(A) has the same meaning given such term in section 201(f) of the Federal Food, Drug, and Cosmetic Act (21 U.S.C. 321(f)); and

(B) includes a dietary supplement as defined in section 201(ff) of such Act.

(6) HEALTH CARE PRACTITIONER- The term `health care practitioner' means a physician or another person who is legally authorized to provide health professional services in the State in which the services are provided.

(7) LABEL- The term `label' has the same meaning given such term in section 201(k) of the Federal Food, Drug, and Cosmetic Act (21 U.S.C. 321(k)) and includes labeling as defined in section 201(m) of such Act (21 U.S.C. 321(m)).

(8) LEGAL REPRESENTATIVE- The term `legal representative' means a parent or an individual who qualifies as a legal guardian under State law.

(9) SELLER- The term `seller' means a person, company, or organization that receives payment related to a medical treatment of a patient of a health practitioner, except that this term does not apply to a health care practitioner who receives payment from an individual or representative of such individual for the administration of a medical treatment to such individual.

(10) MEDICAL TREATMENT- The term `medical treatment' means any food, drug, device, or procedure that is used and intended as a cure, mitigation, treatment, or prevention of disease.

SEC. 3. ACCESS TO MEDICAL TREATMENT.

(a) IN GENERAL- Notwithstanding any other provision of law, and except as provided in subsection (b), an individual shall have the right to be treated by a health care practitioner with any medical treatment (including a medical treatment that is not approved, certified, or licensed by the Secretary of Health and Human Services) that such

275

individual desires or the legal representative of
such individual authorizes if--

(1) such practitioner has personally examined such
individual and agrees to treat such individual; and

(2) the administration of such treatment does not
violate licensing laws.

(b) MEDICAL TREATMENT REQUIREMENTS- A
health care practitioner may provide any medical
treatment to an individual described in subsection
(a) if--

(1) there is no reasonable basis to conclude that the
medical treatment itself, when used as directed, poses
an unreasonable and significant risk of danger to such
individual;

(2) in the case of an individual whose treatment is the
administration of a food, drug, or device that has to be
approved, certified, or licensed by the Secretary of
Health and Human Services, but has not been
approved, certified, or licensed by the Secretary of
Health and Human Services--

(A) such individual has been informed in writing
that such food, drug, or device has not yet been
approved, certified, or licensed by the Secretary of
Health and Human Services for use as a medical
treatment for the condition of such individual;
and

(B) prior to the administration of such treatment,
the practitioner has provided the patient a written
statement that states the following:

`WARNING: This food, drug, or device has not
been declared to be safe and effective by the
Federal Government and any individual who
uses such food, drug, or device, does so at his or
her own risk.';

(3) such individual has been informed in writing of
the nature of the medical treatment, including--

(A) the contents and methods of such treatment;

(B) the anticipated benefits of such treatment;

(C) any reasonably foreseeable side effects that may result from such treatment;

(D) the results of past applications of such treatment by the health care practitioner and others; and

(E) any other information necessary to fully meet the requirements for informed consent of human subjects prescribed by regulations issued by the Food and Drug Administration;

(4) except as provided in subsection (c), there have been no advertising claims made with respect to the efficacy of the medical treatment by the practitioner, manufacturer, or distributor;

(5) the label of any drug, device, or food used in such treatment is not false or misleading; and

(6) such individual--

(A) has been provided a written statement that such individual has been fully informed with respect to the information described in paragraphs (1) through (4);

(B) desires such treatment; and

(C) signs such statement.

In any proceeding relating to the enforcement of paragraph (5) with respect to the label of drugs, devices, or food used in medical treatment covered under this subsection, the provisions of section 403B(c) of the Federal Food, Drug, and Cosmetic Act (21 U.S.C. 343-2(c)) shall apply to establishing the burden of proof that such label is false or misleading.

(c) CLAIM EXCEPTIONS-

(1) REPORTING BY A PRACTITIONER- Subsection (b)(4) shall not apply to an accurate and truthful reporting by a health care practitioner of the results of the practitioner's administration of a medical treatment in recognized journals or at seminars, conventions, or similar meetings or to others so long as the reporting practitioner has no financial interests

in the reporting of the material and has received no financial benefit of any kind from the manufacturer, distributor, or other seller for such reporting. Such reporting may not be used by a manufacturer, distributor, or other seller to advance the sale of such treatment.

(2) STATEMENTS BY A PRACTITIONER TO A PATIENT- Subsection (b)(4) shall not apply to any statement made in person by a health care practitioner to an individual patient or an individual prospective patient.

(3) DIETARY SUPPLEMENTS STATEMENTS- Subsection (b)(4) shall not apply to statements or claims permitted under sections 403B and 403(r)(6) of the Federal Food, Drug, and Cosmetic Act (21 U.S.C. 343-2 and 343(r)(6)).

SEC. 4. REPORTING OF A DANGEROUS MEDICAL TREATMENT.

(a) HEALTH CARE PRACTITIONER- If a health care practitioner, after administering a medical treatment, discovers that the treatment itself was a danger to the individual receiving such treatment, the practitioner shall immediately report to the Secretary of Health and Human Services the nature of such treatment, the results of such treatment, the complete protocol of such treatment, and the source from which such treatment or any part thereof was obtained.

(b) SECRETARY- Upon confirmation that a medical treatment has proven dangerous to an individual, the Secretary of Health and Human Services shall properly disseminate information with respect to the danger of the medical treatment.

SEC. 5. REPORTING OF A BENEFICIAL MEDICAL TREATMENT.

If a health care practitioner, after administering a medical treatment that is not a conventional medical treatment for a life-threatening medical condition or conditions, discovers that, in the opinion of the practitioner, such medical treatment has positive effects on such condition or conditions that are significantly greater than the positive effects that are expected from a conventional medical treatment for the same condition or conditions, the practitioner shall immediately make a reporting, which is accurate and truthful, to the Office of Alternative Medicine of--

(1) the nature of such medical treatment (which is not a conventional medical treatment);

(2) the results of such treatment; and

(3) the protocol of such treatment.

SEC. 6. TRANSPORTATION AND PRODUCTION OF FOOD, DRUGS, DEVICES, AND OTHER EQUIPMENT.

Notwithstanding any other provision of the Federal Food, Drug, and Cosmetic Act (21 U.S.C. 201 et seq.), a person may-

(1) introduce or deliver into interstate commerce a food, drug, device, or any other equipment; and

(2) produce a food, drug, device, or any other equipment, solely for use in accordance with this Act if there have been no advertising claims by the manufacturer, distributor, or seller.

SEC. 7. VIOLATION OF THE CONTROLLED SUBSTANCES ACT.

A health care practitioner, manufacturer, distributor, or other seller may not violate any provision of the Controlled Substances Act (21 U.S.C. 801 et seq.) in the provision of medical treatment in accordance with this Act.

SEC. 8. PENALTY.

A health care practitioner who knowingly violates any provision of this Act shall not be covered by the protections under this Act and shall be subject to all other applicable laws and regulations.

Wake up Americans!

Wake up Americans! The wealth, health and freedom of the 20th century is changing into poverty, sickness and dependency in the 21st century. Our physical and mental deterioration, decreased life expectancy and reduced ability to reproduce are the result of unsuitable foods, adulterated water and the most expensive, poor quality medical care in the world. The cause of our problem is the monopoly that runs our medical care system. It has increased prices faster than the cost of living for 100 years while suppressing advances in medical science that promised lower costs and more benign therapies. The solution was proposed in 1787 by Dr. Benjamin Rush: Constitutional protection of the natural right of Freedom of Choice in Medical Care.

Wake up Americans! Our physical and mental deterioration, decreased life expectancy and reduced ability to reproduce are the result of unsuitable foods, adulterated water and the most expensive, poor quality medical care in the world. Furthermore we can't afford a $2 trillion a year medical bill. For 100 years our medical monopoly has limited our choices, increased prices and suppressed advances in medical science that promised reduced costs. Competition from suppressed technologies can reduce costs. Constitutional protection of the natural right to freedom of choice in medical care, suggested by Dr. Benjamin Rush in 1787, will stimulate competition. State by state ratification of a Rush Amendment is proposed since Congress has proven itself unwilling to control the monopoly.

www.rush2013.com